The Park Avenue Cookbook

THE
PARK AVENUE
COOKBOOK

Sara Stamm

Doubleday & Company, Inc.
Garden City, New York
1981

For
Didi Lorillard
Steven Connell
Ted Peckham

Designed by LAURENCE ALEXANDER

Library of Congress Cataloging in Publication Data

Stamm, Sara B.
The Park Avenue Cookbook.

Includes index.
1. Entertaining. 2. Cookery. I. Title.
TX731.S69   642
ISBN: *0-385-15585-9*
Library of Congress Catalog Card Number 79–6612

CONTENTS

Looking Forward and Looking Back

The planning and pleasures of party giving,
a few fond memories and hints for entertaining.

1

Luncheons

Four winter luncheons, two for spring
and four for summer, all light easy entertaining,
and the pleasant surprise of a midday party.

9

Tea

A peaceful pause in the afternoon, as the mood
changes from day to evening.

47

The Great American Cocktail Party

A few fresh ideas on how to present canapés, pâtés,
cheeses and hot hors d'oeuvre in this
most competitive challenge to the socially active
host or hostess.

57

Romantic Dinners

Six small dinners for the one you love.
Some of these dinner menus are planned for four
guests but they are intended essentially for an
intimate and very special occasion.

73

Dinner at Eight

Eight seated dinner party menus for eight (six
or ten). This chapter considers those times
when formal clothes and carefully planned food
lend glamour and excitement to a
well-chosen guest list.

101

LOOKING FORWARD AND LOOKING BACK

Entertaining is fun. For some people, and I am one of them, it is almost more fun than anything else. It is a challenge and it is also its own reward, for there is nothing nicer than having in your own house (or your garden, your favorite picnic spot or your one-room apartment) the people you care about most. They like you, too, or they wouldn't be there. If the party is organized a little, it will practically run itself and those who enjoy it most may well be the host and hostess.

Of course, the guest list is the key to a successful plan. Once you know that an attractive, mutually interesting group is coming your way, a glowing feeling of anticipation should set in as you look forward to giving them a happy meal in a house smelling of good food with fresh flowers, soft music, flowing wine, candlelight and conversation as added ingredients.

As an aside, I should mention that there are a number of people in everyone's circle who really don't like mingling very much. These shy and fascinating friends should be saved for the pleasant time when you give a party with a guest list of one or two—at the very most four. The little parties can mean as much as the large ones, or more. Some people give parties just to pay back everybody they owe. These occasions can be fun to attend but I prefer to keep my parties more personal.

The selection of a menu is the next step toward the relaxed achievement of your goal, a good party. Plan something interesting and new—perhaps a cold stuffed sea bass, a vegetable pavé, a sorbet of cassis or a hazelnut cream roll—or something that is old and almost forgotten—a crown roast of pork, a steak and kidney pie or a splendid cold English trifle. Often something borrowed turns up, too, because we all pick up ideas from books, restaurants and friends wherever we go. Whatever you do, don't overreach yourself and make your menu so complicated that it will keep you from enjoying yourself. Simple food is just as good as fancy food and a peaceful hostess is more fun than one who is worrying about what is going on in the kitchen.

The truth is that, while food is most important to the success of a good party, the people, the warmth of the welcome that the host and hostess extend, the setting itself, mean almost as much. Good food, food with a knowing flair, is not hard to produce—not rich food, not fancy food, not necessarily expensive food, but just what most of us like, an interesting and satisfying dinner.

Of course, there's no denying it, sometimes *disaster strikes*. Even then, there is a solution. I will cite a few examples.

Last year, one of the most accomplished hostesses in New York invited me among a group of friends for Thanksgiving dinner at her country house outside the city. The guests of honor were two smashing Frenchmen, and my friend went to particular pains to make the feast more wonderful than ever before. A costly fresh-killed turkey was fetched from a nearby farm to crown the board. At four o'clock everything was in readiness, so she went upstairs to dress for dinner, leaving the kitchen in the charge of her maid. We were sipping champagne and nibbling the delectable pâté fresh from Paris, when she came in and murmured in my ear, "The turkey has collapsed!" This hardly seemed believable, but we slipped out to the kitchen to find the dejected bird sprawling defeated in the pan, legs and wings nearly severed from the body. The sight was horrible. A hostess's dilemma! Hoping for the best, we removed all the stuffing and sculpted it into a turkey-shaped mound while a young houseguest rapidly carved the meat into thin slices which, fortunately, were still succulent and juicy (at least the maid had kept basting). We piled the slices symetrically back on the mounded stuffing, stuck the legs back into this effigy at rakish angles and trimmed the unique Thanksgiving bird with ample parsley and strings of cranberries. It really looked rather effective and it tasted absolutely wonderful.

I remember another near-disaster: One summer day in the country, my husband and I were expecting guests for luncheon. The menu was simple: cheese soufflé, chef's salad and a raspberry dessert. As the guests arrived from Woodstock, Vermont, fifty miles away, I went to the kitchen to put the soufflé in the oven. No matter what I tried, the oven simply wouldn't light. Suddenly I remembered that somewhere I had heard of soufflé that was cooked on the top of the stove. I popped mine into a deep pan of warm water, covered it and put it over the flame. We reversed the courses and, while we were eating the salad, the soufflé cooked. It rose and proved a creamy, delicate second course. A new discovery!

Then there was the time that Justin, the dog, ate the steak tartare and . . .

Ah, well, there is one thing about these occasions: you will never forget them.

Mother served lovely food. We grew up in Milton, Massachusetts, and, in those days, four fine meals a day were considered normal. She had been raised in Washington, D.C., which, perhaps, gave her food an added cosmopolitan élan.

For breakfast in New England, besides fruits, oatmeal and ham, creamed codfish might appear. Our luncheons were soufflés, fruit salads or broiled mushrooms and, sometimes, glorious schnecken (baked early in the morning by our nice old German cook). Apparently, all of this delighted my school chums from Milton Academy, who loved to come for lunch and tea.

Teatime provided a much needed respite between field hockey and homework. Piping-hot Lapsang souchong was Mother's favorite, accompanied by little sandwiches, date or butternut bars and plump cookies. Dinner, as I think back, followed a British pattern: puréed soup, a joint of meat with vegetables and, always, hot fresh rolls, puddings or pie with cheese. What pleasant memories good food can conjure up!

At Vassar I majored in art, and the beauty that I discovered there is something that I treasure most among life's blessings. The food, however, was pretty awful and we existed for tea off campus, with gooey chocolate cake and, on our weekend safaris, sizzling steak platters.

But the real genesis for my interest in preparing and presenting fine food came from my husband, J.D. From the moment I met him, he introduced me to the romantic pleasures of New York's beautiful restaurants. Every lunch or dinner was a party: whitebait and oyster crabs with arugula by the duck pond in the courtyard of the old Ritz; pressed duck at Chambord, our old haunt, where the food was prepared behind a glass wall in view of the guests in that wonderful kitchen gleaming with copper pans. There were wiener schnitzel with knodeli, and palatcsinkan at Hapsburg House; we would eat in the little main dining room with its gay Bemelmans murals, where smiling Oscar played the zither, or in the wine cellar, or on the front balcony overlooking Fifty-fifth Street, or on the back balcony overlooking the garden. There were caviar in thin, hot blinis at the Sherry Netherlands under the watchful aegis of our old friend Colonel Serge Obolensky; soft-shell crabs in the garden of the Marguery on Park Avenue at Forty-seventh Street; duck Bigarade at the Paris-Brest; pheasant and crêpes Suzette at "21." J.D. was the initial inspiration for the culinary department of a now very popular restaurant that has become a New York tradition, P. J. Clarke's on Third Avenue. We lived on Sutton Place at Fifty-fifth Street and stopped in there many a noon or night. One day,

J.D. took Mr. Clarke some Dover sole and, right there and then, that accommodating man created for us the first food, besides hard-boiled eggs and pickles, that was ever served in that now hallowed spot. Occasionally, in the spring, we would take the ferry (5¢) with a group of kindred spirits to Hoboken and drink beer and eat steamers—all you could swallow. As I remember, these buttery bivalves were entirely on the house.

But the ultimate grandeurs were on our visits to my husband's Uncle Joe (Joseph E. Davies, who had been ambassador to Russia) and Aunt Marjorie Merriwether Post Davies. On their yacht, in their numerous grand luxe establishments, where footmen slipped silently in and out, or in the great hotels of Europe where long corridors were occupied by the luggage of their entourage, and vendeuses and couriers scampered about like white rabbits, posh was a simple understatement: the palest of caviar, the plumpest of pheasants, gold service, imperial porcelain . . . I blush to remember it.

But to get back to us. For special days, birthdays or anniversary parties, we usually chose Le Pavillon. Its proprietor, Henri Soulé, preferred to plan the menu and wines several days in advance and would discuss the whole affair over a glass or two of champagne. His meals, in the cool, shady garden at the Hedges in Easthampton, were memorable, too. M. Soulé died peacefully in his restaurant after a simple lunch. He lay in state where his friends could bid him farewell in the parish church with a rosary in his hand and the rosette of the Légion d'Honneur in his lapel.

During this time, I came to realize that many of the pleasures of these wonderful establishments could be re-created at home with the added enjoyment of surrounding ourselves with our friends in our own setting. It was marvelous fun to do it, and one way to repay people who really loved food.

In the years that followed, I gathered more ideas, menus and surprises from New York and Europe and incorporated them in this book, written in my apartment overlooking the trees and flowers of Park Avenue.

For me, it's easiest to operate with fairly basic kitchen equipment—good things: skillets, saucepans and bowls of various sizes that stack away neatly, two double boilers, one large and one pint-sized, but not too many gadgets. Wooden spoons and wire whisks of several sizes take up little space and are a godsend.

Among the flourishes that make a party different from just a well-cooked meal, I believe that a pastry tube fitted with various pipes is a treasure. Easy-to-use disposables have recently come on the market. Give yourself and your cook a practice session or two and you'll see what a difference it makes in the look of all sorts of desserts, eggs and canapés. The present-day tube in common use is equipped with a plastic sack and is a cinch to operate and clean, and it gushes out lovely dollops of fluted cream, frosting, pâté and puréed vegetables.

A tip from professional and near-professionals that should not be overlooked has been brought to my attention by Martin Shallenberger, one of Park Avenue's favorite bachelor hosts when he isn't traveling the seas on the *Shalimar* or at his Schloss Eferding in Austria. He suggests using, occasionally, a t i n y drop of food coloring to heighten the appearance of certain dishes. Food colorings are tasteless and pure. A small drop of red can enhance the appearance of a shrimp soup or a fruit dessert. Just a drop of green may help to make a sauce verte look its best and can be used with subtle effect. Remember, a t i n y drop.

Among the silent servants on the cooking scene, there are some I couldn't live without. They deserve their counter space and are used continually, saving time and money; they achieve wonderful results. There is, first, the indispensable Mixmaster for mixing beautifully light cakes and beating eggs and cream to exact perfection. The food processor has produced a culinary revolution that has made it possible to prepare vegetables shredded in various attractive ways, either raw or marinated in interesting oils and vinegars or lightly cooked and still tasting of their own sweet selves, to prepare pâtés of meats or vegetables with incredible ease, to mix light, perfect pastry in a whiz. New York's restaurants rely heavily on this miracle worker for their ever increasing innovations.

Lastly, I am a fan who is sold on the turbo oven, which sits cosily beside the big gas range and does twice as much duty as the old-fashioned indispensable oven. It works more quickly because the air within the oven is in constant circulation, and you can peek through the glass door at eye level to see just how things fare with the roast or the soufflé or the popovers. Both it and the Cuisinart make the annual trip to Easthampton and back to New York as honored passengers.

The menus that make up this book are those that I have used with great success and they have earned me many compliments. Some are more or less expensive, some are as economical as today's markets can provide but, I think, not less interesting. I have planned them all so that they can be presented with, at most, one servant. Lots of them you can do yourself. I prefer not to have too many friends "helping" in the kitchen and, if they show leanings in that direction, it's best to give them little tasks like opening the wine, lighting the candles or freshening a drink for someone.

This book is presented in the form of menus for planning convenience. Here are menus for the four seasons, for occasions great and small. There are romantic dinners for two, menus for dress-up, sit-down dinners at eight and for other celebrations and hours. Recipes are furnished for all dishes that are not available in standard cookbooks.

In general, these may be followed exactly with excellent results, but the interested cook should feel free to make changes as expediency or taste suggests. Once you get interested, experimenting is half the fun.

My thanks are due to many friends besides those special three to whom this book is, in gratitude, dedicated: to Louise Gault, my editor, whose remarkable understanding of good food is famous; to Marianne Strong, my friend and my literary agent, whose enthusiasm and taste are reflected in every chapter; to Susan Carey, who cooked her way through lots of it, encouraging me in moments of despair; to Marjorie White, Tom Kefalis and Tom Walsh, who put everything together with knowing skill and, last, to my dear friend, Eve Hatch Holmes. She read the whole thing through and gave me the benefit of all the wisdom she had acquired in her years as fashion editor of *Town and Country*. *Yankee Magazine*, that prodigy of New England publishing, has kindly given me permission to include some recipes that I used in the book I did for them, *Favorite New England Recipes* (Yankee Inc., Dublin, N.H., 1971). Friends gave recipes with happy generosity and their names appear above them in the pages that follow. I thank you all very much.

LUNCHEONS

A luncheon party is particular fun. At a relaxed, informal time of day with no stress or pressure, a midday party can be something of a novelty to break the everyday routine.

Guests are inclined to be delightfully punctual, which, alas, is not quite so sure to be the case in the evening; the time allotted to cocktails is briefer. So, at lunch, a soufflé can be planned without the fear of a delay which can be fatal to this light and dependable dish. This chapter, therefore, contains several soufflés. Luncheon menus and the setting, too, can be more varied than parties at dinner time and a picnicky atmosphere prevails. People can be invited on rather shorter notice than at dinner time when the world seems to get so busy.

I find luncheon parties can be immensely popular occasions when even the busiest people are apt to settle down for a couple of hours with a happy feeling of playing hookey from the more serious affairs of life.

Four Winter Luncheons

MENU I
SERVES 6

Fresh Asparagus
Sauce Maltese

Lobster Soufflé
Bell Peppers Stuffed with Corn
Sour Cream Muffins

Green Figs Vanderbilt
Pecan Puffs

Bolla Trebbiano

SAUCE MALTESE

This recipe for Sauce Maltese is quickly made in the food processor or blender. With the processor use the steel blade.

3 egg yolks
2 tablespoons orange juice
grated rind of 1 orange
¼ teaspoon dry mustard
dash cayenne pepper
¼ pound butter (1 stick)
salt to taste

Put the egg yolks in the receptacle and beat until lemon-colored. Add the orange juice and rind, mustard and cayenne. Process. Heat the butter to the boiling point and immediately turn on the motor of the machine and pour in the butter in a thin, steady stream. Add salt to taste. Serve immediately over fresh asparagus or keep warm in a bain-marie or double boiler. (This sauce is good, too, on broccoli and cauliflower.)

LOBSTER SOUFFLÉ

SERVES 6

6 tablespoons butter
6 tablespoons flour
3 cups milk
salt
white pepper
dash cayenne
6 egg yolks
2 cups lobster meat, diced
9 egg whites
butter for soufflé dish

Preheat oven to 400° F.

Over a low flame, melt the butter; stir in the flour and gradually add all of the milk. Stir until the mixture is smooth and thick. Add the seasoning. Remove from heat. Cool a little and beat in the egg yolks one at a time. Add the lobster meat and stir to blend. Beat the egg whites until stiff but not dry and, with a rubber spatula, fold them gently into the lobster mixture. Divide between two buttered 1-quart soufflé dishes. Bake for 25–30 minutes until puffed and golden brown. Serve at once.

BELL PEPPERS STUFFED WITH CORN

SERVES 10

CREAMED CORN

2 cups corn
2 tablespoons butter
¼ cup heavy cream
salt to taste
pinch cayenne pepper

Boil corn on the cob, 6–8 ears, depending on size, until just tender to yield 2 cups kernels. Purée corn in blender or food processor for about 1 minute until corn is quite smooth. To the puréed corn add the butter, cream, salt and cayenne pepper. Blend briefly to mix. Set aside to stuff peppers.

GREEN PEPPERS

10 small green peppers
20 fresh basil leaves

Preheat oven to 350° F.

Parboil green peppers with the tops cut out and seeds scooped out. Stuff each green pepper with the creamed corn mixture. Place stuffed peppers on cookie sheet and bake for 5–10 minutes depending on size of peppers.

Garnish with coarsely chopped fresh basil leaves, which are usually available in the market. Only fresh basil leaves make this recipe work.

SOUR CREAM MUFFINS*

12 (2-INCH) MUFFINS

2 cups flour
1 teaspoon baking powder
½ teaspoon baking soda
½ teaspoon salt
3 tablespoons sugar
1 egg, well beaten
1¼ cups sour cream

Preheat oven to 425° F.

Sift the dry ingredients together. Mix the egg and sour cream. Stir the egg mixture into the flour mixture, *quickly*. This is the secret of tender muffins. Turn immediately into greased muffin tins, filling them half full. Bake for 15–20 minutes. Serve hot from the oven with curls of sweet butter.

GREEN FIGS VANDERBILT

SERVES 6

Mrs. Murray Vanderbilt's recipe.

18 fresh figs, halved
Armagnac
sour cream
finely shredded orange rind

Arrange the figs in a shallow bowl. Cover the bottom of the bowl with about ½ inch Armagnac. Chill. Put dollops of sour cream on the figs and sprinkle with orange rind.

*Courtesy of Yankee Magazine, "Favorite New England Recipes" by Sara B. Stamm, Yankee Inc., Dublin, New Hampshire, 1971.

PECAN PUFFS

Mrs. Stephen Sanford, superhostess of Palm Beach and Saratoga, has given me some of her most successful recipes. These cookies are rich perfection.

1 cup shelled pecans, ground
1 cup sifted cake flour
½ cup butter, softened and beaten smooth
2 tablespoons granulated sugar, added to butter until creamy
powdered sugar for garnish

Preheat oven to 300° F.

Stir pecans and flour into butter mixture. Roll dough into small balls. Place on greased baking sheet. Bake for 25 minutes. Roll while hot in powdered sugar. (Note: These burn very easily, so check them while they are baking.)

Squash Soup
Corn Sticks

Veal Chops with Endive Sauce
Baked Pears Stuffed with Spinach

Brandied Peaches
Crêpes Hélène

An *Austrian white wine* would be exceptionally flattering to this luncheon. I have a weakness for the beautiful wines of Austria, whose vineyards, strung along the north side of the Danube, are among the oldest and finest in the world and yet are not very well known in this country. Martin Shallenberger lives at Schloss Eferding on the Danube near Linz. It was there that I first learned to love these captivating wines. Durnstein, where Richard Lion-Heart was held captive, Krems Sandgrube and the Ausberger vineyards at Strass produce light brilliant wines. Muller Thurgrau's Kabinett wine has a robust quality of the earth.

The prices of these fine wines are remarkable in view of their very high quality. The vineyards are small so any given variety is not always available. You will find others at your wine merchant which will be a pleasure to try.

SQUASH SOUP

SERVES 6

A comforting and healthy winter dish.

2 cups fresh purée of acorn squash, seasoned to taste
1 cup heavy cream
3 cups chicken stock

½ cup salted whipped cream
¼ cup chopped toasted hazelnuts
fresh nutmeg

Combine the squash, cream and stock in a saucepan, stir well and bring to the boil. Serve hot, garnished with salted whipped cream and chopped toasted hazelnuts. Pass a nutmeg grater with the soup.

CORN STICKS

14 CORN STICKS

1 cup cornmeal
1 cup all-purpose flour
¼ cup sugar
3 teaspoons baking powder
1 teaspoon salt
1 egg, well beaten
1 cup milk
¼ cup melted butter

Preheat the oven to 425° F.

Sift together the dry ingredients. Mix the egg, milk and melted butter separately and combine the two mixtures lightly. Half fill well-greased corn-stick pans* and bake for 15–20 minutes. Serve with plenty of sweet butter.

* Cast-aluminum pans are made expressly for these sticks and produce a pretty little bread. Lacking them, use muffin pans instead.

VEAL CHOPS WITH ENDIVE SAUCE

SERVES 6

6 large loin veal chops
salt and freshly grated pepper
Endive Sauce (recipe follows)

Preheat the broiler.

Season the chops and then grill them on one side on the rack close to the heat for 3 or 4 minutes. Give the chops a half turn and grill for a few minutes longer, making a seared crisscross pattern on the chops. Turn and cook on other side until done. Arrange the chops on a hot platter with the cross pattern on top. Pour Endive Sauce around the chops and serve.

ENDIVE SAUCE

SERVES 6

6 heads Belgian endive
4 tablespoons butter
1 tablespoon lemon juice
salt to taste
1 teaspoon sugar
freshly ground white pepper
2 cups heavy cream

Wipe the endives clean and trim the ends. Cut crosswise in ¼-inch slices. Melt the butter in a skillet with the lemon juice. Sauté the endives until tender, about 10 minutes, adding salt, sugar and pepper. Do not use an aluminum utensil as it discolors endive. Add the cream. Cook gently for 10 minutes more and pour around the chops.

BAKED PEARS STUFFED WITH SPINACH

SERVES 6

1 pound fresh spinach, puréed or 1 package frozen puréed spinach
salt, pepper and nutmeg to taste
3 tablespoons sour cream
3 large Bosc pears
3 long-stemmed cloves
juniper berries

Preheat oven to 350° F.

Cook the spinach and squeeze it dry. Purée, season and mix with sour cream and stuff in center of halved, peeled and pitted pears, leaving the stem on one half of each pear and inserting a long clove, stemlike, in the other half. Bake for 20–30 minutes. Serve garnished with juniper berries.

CRÊPES HÉLÈNE

SERVES 6

All-Purpose Crêpe Batter (recipe follows)
butter or oil
½ pint heavy cream
½ teaspoon vanilla extract
sugar to taste
Chocolate Sauce (recipe follows)
pistachio nuts

Pour 2 or 3 tablespoons of Crêpe Batter into an omelette or crêpe pan which has been oiled or buttered and heated over medium heat. Lift the pan above the heating unit and tilt it in all directions so the bottom of the pan is covered with a very thin layer of batter. Return to heat and cook crêpe until the bottom side is browned, then carefully turn with a spatula. Brown other side for a few seconds. Remove from pan and repeat. Stack crêpes on a plate in a warm oven. Whip, flavor and sweeten the cream and store in the refrigerator. Prepare the Chocolate Sauce and chop the nuts.

At serving time, roll each crêpe around a dollop of whipped cream. Arrange 2 per person on a warm plate. Cover with hot Chocolate Sauce and garnish with chopped pistachio nuts.

ALL-PURPOSE CRÊPE BATTER

18 CRÊPES

2 eggs
pinch salt
1 cup flour
1⅛ cups milk
⅛ cup melted butter

In a mixing bowl, combine the eggs and salt. Beat until well blended, gradually adding the flour alternately with the milk. Beat in the melted butter. Refrigerate for at least an hour before using. Extra batter can be saved and used later.

CHOCOLATE SAUCE

1 CUP

2 squares unsweetened chocolate
½ cup black coffee
⅓ cup sugar
2 tablespoons butter
½ teaspoon vanilla extract or other flavoring

Melt the chocolate in the coffee over very low heat or in a double boiler, stirring until slightly thickened. Stir in the butter, sugar and vanilla or liqueur flavoring: a little crème de menthe, kirsch, brandy or rum lends character to the sauce.

(This devastatingly rich sauce will stiffen when poured over ice cream.)

MENU III

FOR 8

Apple Soup

Paillard of Chicken
Tomato Salad with Basil
Artichoke Bottoms Stuffed with Duxelles
Popovers

Hazelnut Cream Roll

A White Burgundy

APPLE SOUP

SERVES 8

Subtle and refreshing, this is a recipe of the late Elizabeth Arden Graham.

1 large onion, chopped
4 stalks celery, chopped
3 tablespoons butter
3 large green apples, peeled, cored and sliced
3 cups beef bouillon
3 cups chicken bouillon
1 teaspoon curry powder
1 teaspoon paprika
juice of 1 lemon
½ cup heavy cream

Preheat oven to 350° F.

Sauté the chopped onion and celery in the butter until golden brown. Add the apples and cook in the oven for 20 minutes in a covered pan. Add the beef and chicken bouillons, the curry powder, paprika and lemon juice. Season to taste, strain and bring to the boil. Remove from the heat and finally add the heavy cream. Serve immediately.

PAILLARD OF CHICKEN

The easy elegance of this dish makes it an invaluable addition to your repertoire. Surround it with lemon halves tied in tulle and lots of fresh, curly parsley and it will look as fine as it tastes. (Ten pieces to serve 8 people.)

5 chicken breasts, each cut in half, boned and skinned
1 cup pulverized almonds
1 tablespoon grated zest of lemon
¼ pound butter (1 stick)
1 jigger cognac
3 tablespoons whole green Madagascar peppercorns
½ cup heavy cream
lemon halves and parsley for garnish

Flatten the chicken breasts by covering them with plastic wrap and beating them with a mallet. Dip each one in the almond crumbs mixed with the lemon zest to coat well. At this point, the chicken may be stored in the refrigerator until needed. Before serving, sauté the pieces in sweet butter until the crusts are golden brown. Arrange on a hot platter. Deglaze the pan juices with the cognac. Add the peppercorns and cream and stir together. Pour this sauce over the paillard and garnish with lemon halves and parsley.

ARTICHOKE BOTTOMS STUFFED WITH DUXELLES

SERVES 8

1 pound mushrooms
3 tablespoons butter
salt, pepper and paprika to taste
10 artichoke bottoms, fresh cooked
parsley

Wash and trim the mushrooms. Mince them very fine and squeeze dry in a clean cloth. Cook them in the butter over low heat until all their juices are cooked away. Season to taste with salt, pepper and a little paprika and again squeeze the mixture dry. Spoon hot into the artichoke bottoms and keep warm until serving time. Serve garnished with parsley.

POPOVERS

10 POPOVERS

butter for cups or tins
4 eggs
2 cups milk
2 cups flour
¼ teaspoon salt

Preheat oven to 425° F.

Butter 10 earthenware cups or muffin tins generously. Set in the oven. Stir the ingredients together but do not beat; the batter should be a bit lumpy. Divide the batter among the heated buttered cups or tins and bake for about 45 minutes until the popovers are puffed and firm. Prick each with a knife to allow steam to escape and serve at once.

It is not hard to make high, puffy popovers; their appearance is impressive and always seems to bring a sign of joy. Actually, they can be started in a cold oven that is then turned to 425° F., but the cooking is faster if the oven and cups have been preheated. If you wish to slow down their cooking, the oven temperature may be lowered after they have popped.

HAZELNUT CREAM ROLL

6 egg yolks
¾ cup sugar
1½ cups hazelnuts, ground
2 teaspoons baking powder
pinch salt
6 egg whites
2 pints heavy cream, whipped

Preheat oven to 375° F.

Beat the egg yolks and the sugar in electric mixer or food processor until the mixture forms ribbons when dropped from the beaters. Add the ground nuts mixed with the baking powder and salt. Beat the egg whites until stiff but not dry, and gently fold the egg whites into the nut mixture. Spread on buttered waxed paper on a buttered cookie sheet and bake for 15–20 minutes until it tests done. Remove and cover the surface immediately with a towel dipped in cold water and wrung out. Place in the refrigerator to cool. When the bottom of the cookie sheet is cool turn the roll onto two overlapping pieces of waxed paper and carefully remove the paper on which it was baked. Spread the surface with whipped cream, roll up and refrigerate until needed.

MENU IV

Persimmons with Horseradish Sauce

Swordfish Gratinée
Small Boiled New Potatoes in Chive Butter
Salad of Greens
French Bread

Soufflé Harlequin with Whipped Cream

A Bolla Soave, dry and very compatible with fish

PERSIMMONS WITH HORSERADISH SAUCE

SERVES 4

An amusing and attractive first course, this recipe was given to me by my friend Henry Munson, a New York bachelor with a great flair for entertaining. It sounds funny, but it isn't. It's delicious.

4 ripe persimmons
3 ounces grated horseradish, drained
pinch dry mustard
½ pint heavy cream, whipped

Set the persimmons upright on individual plates. Stir the horseradish and mustard into the whipped cream and pass in a sauce dish. This is a first course that can be placed on the table in advance and looks spectacular.

SWORDFISH GRATINÉE

SERVES 4

1 swordfish steak, 2 pounds
¼ cup seasoned bread crumbs
¼ cup pistachio or hazelnut crumbs
¼ pound butter (1 stick)
chopped chives
4 lemon halves for garnish
parsley for garnish

Bring the swordfish to room temperature and cover both sides with a mixture of the bread crumbs and nut crumbs. In a large pan, sauté the fish in butter, covered at first so that it will cook through. Turn carefully and cook until done. Cover with chopped chives and serve surrounded with lemon halves and parsley.

SOUFFLÉ HARLEQUIN WITH WHIPPED CREAM

1 (1-QUART) SOUFFLÉ

This soufflé, half chocolate and half vanilla, makes a pretty and amusing dessert.

butter and sugar for soufflé dish
2 tablespoons butter
2 tablespoons flour
¾ cup milk
½ cup sugar
pinch salt
4 egg yolks, lightly beaten
1 square semi-sweet chocolate
1 tablespoon cold coffee
½ teaspoon vanilla extract
5 egg whites
½ pint heavy cream, whipped, sweetened and flavored with
    ½ teaspoon vanilla extract

Preheat the oven to 375° F.

Butter a soufflé dish and sprinkle the bottom and sides with sugar. Melt the 2 tablespoons butter in a saucepan and stir in the flour. Gradually stir in the milk with a wire whisk and continue stirring the mixture until it thickens. Add the ½ cup sugar and the salt. Add the egg yolks and stir together gently. Divide this sauce into 2 parts. Melt the chocolate with the coffee over hot water and add to one half of the egg sauce; to the other half add the vanilla extract.

Beat the egg whites until they form stiff, glossy peaks. Fold one half of them into the chocolate mixture, half into the vanilla. Fill the soufflé dish with alternate large spoonfuls of the two mixtures. Bake until puffed and browned—30–45 minutes. Serve at once with chilled whipped cream.

MENU I

FOR 4

Green Asparagus, Mousseline Sauce
Shad Roe with Sorrel Sauce, Crisp Bacon Garnish
Dilled New Potatoes
French Bread

Strawberries Jupiter
Homemade Sugar Cookies

A white Burgundy or Vouvray

NOTE If sorrel is unobtainable, Endive Sauce (*see Index*) is a tart and pleasant substitute.

MOUSSELINE SAUCE

ABOUT 1½ CUPS

To 1 cup Hollandaise Sauce (recipe follows) add ½ cup whipped cream.

HOLLANDAISE SAUCE

ABOUT 1 CUP

3 egg yolks
1 tablespoon water
¼ pound butter (1 stick)
juice ½ lemon
salt
dash cayenne pepper

In an earthenware bowl or in the top of a double boiler over hot water (never let the water come to a boil), blend the egg yolks and water with a wire whisk until fluffy. Add the butter ⅓ stick at a time, blending well after each addition. Then add the lemon juice and seasonings. Stir the mixture constantly until it is thick.

If the sauce should curdle from overheating you can rescue it by removing it immediately from the heat and adding a tablespoon of very hot water or a tablespoon of chilled cream. An ice cube can also be used; remove it as soon as the sauce becomes smooth. Be cautious in reheating the sauce. It is not difficult to make Hollandaise, as many people believe, but really quite easy.

SORREL SAUCE

ABOUT ¾ CUP

½ pound sorrel leaves
2 tablespoons sour cream
1 tablespoon red currant or pear vinegar
salt
lemon pepper

Pick over the sorrel leaves; remove stems and wash and dry the leaves. Purée. In a small saucepan, heat them with the sour cream and vinegar. Season to taste with a little salt and lemon pepper.

STRAWBERRIES JUPITER

Ever since my sister, Mrs. Thomas Turner, adopted this from the Jupiter Island Club it has been our springtime special.

1½ quarts fresh strawberries
¼–½ cup sugar
1 (10-ounce) package frozen raspberries, defrosted
1 tablespoon orange liqueur
1 teaspoon lemon juice
½ cup chopped pistachio nuts
sprigs fresh mint

Wash and hull the strawberries and dry them on paper toweling. Slice them, cover with sugar, and chill for several hours. Purée the raspberries in a blender and strain them to remove the seeds. Add the orange liqueur and lemon juice and chill. Just before serving, ladle over the strawberries and garnish with pistachio nuts and sprigs of mint.

MENU II

Fruits au Kirsch

Soft-Shell Crabs Amandines
Zucchini Fritters with Tomatoes
Young Lettuce with Herbs, Dressed with Cream

Garlic-Cheese Sticks

Rhubarb Pie

Iced Moselle

SOFT-SHELL CRABS AMANDINES

SERVES 6

12 soft-shell crabs
flour
salt and freshly ground black pepper
8 tablespoons butter (1 stick)
1 teaspoon Worcestershire sauce
3 teaspoons minced parsley
½ cup blanched sliced almonds
lemon halves for garnish

Rinse the crabs. Lift their shells and scrape out the spongy area between the shell and flesh. Cut off the tails. Dry the crabs and dip in flour seasoned with salt and freshly ground black pepper. Fry quickly on each side in the butter until golden. Arrange on hot plates. Add Worcestershire sauce, minced parsley and blanched almonds to the butter and sauté until the almonds are browned. Pour over the crabs and serve with lemon halves which have been tied in net.

ZUCCHINI FRITTERS WITH TOMATOES

1 pound zucchini
2 teaspoons salt
1 egg
2 teaspoons minced onion
2–3 tablespoons dry bread crumbs
vegetable oil
4 large tomatoes, halved

Scrub, trim and grate the zucchini. Sprinkle it with the salt and place in a large collander. Let it drain for 30 minutes, then put it into a dish towel and squeeze dry. In a bowl, beat the egg until light; add the zucchini, minced onion and enough bread crumbs to absorb all the moisture. At this point, the mixture can be stored until needed. When ready to serve, heat enough oil to measure ½ inch deep in a heavy skillet and drop the zucchini mixture in by tablespoons. Fry on both sides until crisp. Drain on paper toweling and serve with halved tomatoes which have been fried in the same pan.

RHUBARB PIE

1 (9-INCH) PIE

The very taste of spring is in the first old-fashioned rhubarb pie.

Pastry for a Double-Crust Pie (recipe follows)
1½ cups of sugar
¼ cup cornstarch
¼ teaspoon salt
1 pound rhubarb, cut in 1½-inch lengths (discard the tops, which are
    poisonous)
2 teaspoons grated orange rind, or 1 teaspoon grated lemon rind
juice of 1 orange

1 drop red food coloring (optional)
2 tablespoons butter
milk
sugar

Preheat oven to 400° F.

Divide the pastry into uneven halves. Roll out the larger portion and fit into a 9-inch pie pan. Trim the pastry ½ inch beyond the rim of the pan. Roll out the remaining pastry to ⅛-inch thickness and cut in strips about ¾ inch wide. Sprinkle the bottom crust with a tablespoon of the sugar. This will cook quickly, forming a coating which prevents the bottom crust from becoming soggy. Mix the rest of the sugar, the cornstarch and the salt. Add the rhubarb, citrus rind and juice and toss until well mixed. Tint pink, if desired, and turn into the pastry shell. Dot with butter. Arrange the pastry strips over the pie in a lattice pattern, securing them to the pie shell firmly and fluting the pie shell and strips together to form a high rim. Brush the pastry with a little milk and sprinkle sugar over it. Bake for 50–60 minutes until the filling has bubbles that do not break. Serve a little warm.

PASTRY FOR A DOUBLE-CRUST PIE

ENOUGH FOR A 9-INCH PIE

The perfect formula.

1¾ cups flour
1 teaspoon salt
⅔ cup Crisco
⅓ cup ice water

Put the flour, salt and Crisco in the food processor and process until crumbly. Add the ice water. When the dough gathers into a ball remove and chill in the refrigerator before rolling.

MENU I

FOR 6–8

A few years ago we spent a hot, golden summer at Porto Santo Stefano, that tiny promontory north of Rome where Italians love to while away July and August. The outstanding hostess in this merry resort was Lily Gerini, who lived in a cool white marble villa high over the blue Tyrrhenian Sea on the same spot where Nero (none other) summered some years ago. It is said by Chimider Suetonius, that the Emperor was so addicted to cool ices that he kept relays of slaves running from the Alps to bring snow for his sherbets. Life is simpler now and Countess Gerini's luncheon, which was, but for minor variations, almost always about the same, seemed to me perfect for the hot Italian days. I have adapted it and used it many times, an ideal menu for midday in warm weather. First there were Bloody Marys (made with fresh *pomodori*) on the little beach by the water's edge, then we climbed up to the cool rooms where parts of *La Dolce Vita* had been filmed. There her smiling footmen in pink-and-white striped cotton coats served us lunch.

Gnocchi alla Romana

Cold Stuffed Striped Bass
Cucumber Sauce
Italian Bread

Fresh Pineapple Mousse

Chilled Frascati or Orvieto wine
And afterward, on a cliff overlooking the serene seascape;
Hot Café Filtre and mints.

GNOCCHI ALLA ROMANA

The recipe is easy to double for larger parties.

1 cup farina
2 cups milk
1 teaspoon salt

Cook together for 15 minutes, stirring continually in the top of a double boiler. Remove and add:

2 slightly beaten egg whites
1 tablespoon butter
¼ cup finely grated fresh Parmesan cheese

Beat well and refrigerate overnight.

Preheat oven to 375° F.

Roll the dough out on a floured board to a thickness of about ½ inch. Cut into 2½-inch rounds and lay in a buttered shallow baking dish, one round overlapping another. Sprinkle with more Parmesan, dot with butter and bake until neatly browned. Pass more grated Parmesan with the gnocchi.

COLD STUFFED STRIPED BASS

SERVES 6–8

1 (5-pound) striped bass, cooked and boned
3 hard-boiled eggs
1 pound mushrooms
olive oil
salt and pepper to taste
chopped hearts of 1 bunch celery
1 tablespoon minced chives
3 tablespoons capers

GARNISH

avacodo and tomato slices
watercress
lemon halves

Have the bass cooked and boned by your fish market. Place the following stuffing between the two halves of the fish.

Chop the eggs fine. Chop the mushrooms and sauté them in a frying pan in olive oil with salt and pepper. Mix these together with the celery, chives and capers.

Chill the stuffed fish until serving time. Garnish the chilled platter before serving.

CUCUMBER SAUCE

2 cucumbers, peeled, diced and drained
1 cup heavy cream, whipped
½ cup mayonnaise
¼ cup capers, drained
Dijon mustard to taste

Combine and serve with cold fish or use to mask fish.

FRESH PINEAPPLE MOUSSE

2 eggs
½ cup sugar
2 cups puréed fresh pineapple
3 cups heavy cream
pinch salt

Beat the eggs until light. Beat the cream with the salt until stiff. Gradually beat the sugar into the eggs and combine with the pineapple and the whipped cream. Freeze in an ice-cream freezer or use the freezer unit in your refrigerator, beating the mixture when it is half frozen.

Cold Cherry Soup

Sliced Cold Roast Lamb with Cumberland Sauce 1
New Peas à la Française
Buttered Noodles with Slivers of Prosciutto
Hot Herbed French Bread

French Cheeses
Pears, Figs and Cranshaw Melons

Cella Lambrusca

Caffè Espresso

Roast the leg of lamb according to the recipe (*see Index*) for Roast Lamb au Jus. This may be done a day in advance. Chill, slice and serve tender and pink.

On a hot day, Cella Lambrusca is the perfect accompaniment. This pleasantly priced light red Italian wine is delicious and is best served chilled.

COLD CHERRY SOUP

SERVES 10

Some years ago whe she was only a precocious child, Didi Lorillard, who lives in New York and Newport, gave me this lovely summer recipe. "Yum yum," it says in her girlish hand. Since then she has produced a book, *New York City Slicker*, a very savvy guide to things hereabouts, and a fat, bouncing baby, Olivia Lorillard Cowley. She is also the godmother of this book. She smiled sweetly and twisted my arm ever so gently until it came out of the typewriter and onto the printed page.

1½ quarts pitted sour cherries
½ cup water
sugar to taste
3 cups heavy cream
cinnamon

Chop the cherries and simmer them in their juices with the· water, sugar and 1½ cups of the cream for 10 to 15 minutes. Chill overnight. Before serving, fold in remaining cream, and dust lightly with cinnamon.

CUMBERLAND SAUCE I

ABOUT 1 CUP

This is the authentic Cumberland Sauce. I have adapted it from an old recipe of Escoffier. Nothing could taste better as an accompaniment for game, fowl or lamb dishes.

½ cup red currant jelly
3 jiggers port wine
2 teaspoons shallots, finely chopped and blanched
rind of 1 orange cut in julienne strips
rind of 1 lemon cut in julienne strips
juice of 2 oranges
juice of ½ lemon
2 teaspoons dry mustard
powdered ginger to taste
cayenne pepper to taste

Mix all ingredients well over low heat and serve hot or cold.

NEW PEAS À LA FRANÇAISE

One of the finest treats of summer is a mess of tiny green peas picked and shelled the morning that they are eaten. This is an ideal way to cook them.

4 pounds fresh peas
5 or 6 green lettuce leaves
a few snips of fresh thyme or mint
2 tablespoons water
salt and freshly ground white pepper
1 level teaspoon sugar
4 tablespoons or more sweet butter
sprigs of mint for garnish
1 tablespoon additional butter

Shell the peas and place in a heavy iron or earthenware pot on a bed of lettuce leaves. Add the other ingredients, cover closely and cook over low heat until the peas are tender and still moist. Remove the lettuce leaves and discard them. Add more butter to suit your taste. Pile in a hot serving dish, garnish with sprigs of mint and another pat of butter.

MENU III

This is a typically American luncheon for a lovely summer day.

Chilled Curried Melon Balls

Cold Roast Chicken
Chutney
Spinach Salad with Anchovy Dressing
Blueberry Popovers
Sweet Butter

Fresh Raspberry Shortcake
or
Fresh Peach Shortcake
Whipped Cream

A cold white vin ordinaire *or iced tea with mint and lime*

CHILLED CURRIED MELON BALLS

SERVES 8

Curry Sauce (recipe follows)
mint for garnish

Arrange chilled melon balls in individual glass dishes, top with a dollop of Curry Sauce and garnish with mint.

½ cup sour cream
½ teaspoon curry paste
1 teaspoon lemon juice
chopped candied ginger to taste
salt to taste

Stir together and chill.

SPINACH SALAD WITH ANCHOVY DRESSING

SERVES 8

1 small can anchovy fillets, mashed
French dressing
2 pounds spinach leaves
chopped chives
1 bunch radishes, trimmed and sliced
¼ pound mushrooms, sliced
½ pound bacon, cooked until crisp and crumbled
freshly made buttered garlic croutons (optional)

Mash the anchovies and mix them into the French dressing. Wash and dry the spinach leaves and toss them in the dressing with the chives, radishes and mushrooms. Garnish with the bacon. Garlic croutons may be added to this salad if you want to make it more substantial.

BLUEBERRY POPOVERS

10 POPOVERS

Using the recipe for Popovers (*see Index*), add ½ cup blueberries, lightly sugared, to the batter. The berries will burst, hot, juicy and succulent.

FRESH RASPBERRY SHORTCAKE

SERVES 10

The best of all shortcakes, I feel, with peach running a close second, this one is made in the proper old-fashioned way with short biscuit dough.

½ cup shortening (Crisco is good)
3 cups flour sifted with:
  4 teaspoons baking powder
  1 teaspoon salt
  1 teaspoon sugar
1⅛ cups milk
sweet butter
2 quarts raspberries at room temperature
sugar
1 pint heavy cream, whipped

Preheat oven to 425° F.

With fork or fingers blend the shortening into the dry ingredients, and little by little stir in the milk to form a soft dough. Turn onto a floured board and pat into one large layer. Bake for 15–18 minutes. Split carefully into two layers and butter the halves. Meanwhile, pick over the berries and, reserving a few for garnish, sweeten lightly. Lightly whip the cream and sweeten very lightly. Chill. Put the prepared fruit between the layers of warm shortcake, cover with the chilled whipped cream, garnish with saved berries and serve.

MENU IV

Cucumber Yogurt Soup

Crusty Rolls, Split, Toasted and Buttered
Salade Argenteuil
Red Wine Basil Vinaigrette Sauce
Mélange of Summer Vegetables, Mayonnaise

Blueberry Crumble
Whipped Cream

A chilled Spanish Rioja would be refreshing with this informal lunch, and espresso with a twist of lemon peel a nice contrast with the crumble.

CUCUMBER YOGURT SOUP

SERVES 8

4 cucumbers
2 cloves garlic, crushed
1 pint chicken stock
1 pint yogurt
salt and pepper
½ cup chopped walnuts
finely chopped chives

Peel the cucumbers, quarter them, remove the seeds and slice thin. Add the other ingredients except the nuts and chives and chill for several hours. When ready to serve, stir in the nut meats and garnish with chives.

SALADE ARGENTEUIL

*2 or 3 heads various salad greens, washed and dried and torn into
    bite-size pieces*
vinaigrette dressing
*3 pounds rare shell roast beef, cut into julienne strips about ¼ inch
    thick*
2 pounds fresh string beans cut into julienne strips and cooked al dente
2 tablespoons minced shallots
½ bunch parsley, minced
4 tablespoons capers for garnish
Red Wine Basil Vinaigrette Sauce (recipe follows)

Toss the salad greens in enough vinaigrette sauce to coat the leaves thoroughly. Mix the roast beef, green beans, shallots and parsley separately in more vinaigrette sauce and arrange all in a large salad bowl. Garnish with capers.

RED WINE BASIL VINAIGRETTE SAUCE

ABOUT 1 CUP

¾ cup olive oil
6 tablespoons red wine basil vinegar
½ teaspoon salt
⅛ teaspoon ground pepper
1 teaspoon Dijon mustard
1 whole clove garlic

Combine all ingredients in a container; shake.

MÉLANGE OF SUMMER VEGETABLES
MAYONNAISE

Pick an assortment of young vegetables from the garden or farmer's market: cauliflower, peas, lima beans, baby carrots, cucumber, new beets or white radishes. Prepare them in bite-size pieces, breaking the cauliflower into flowerets, peeling, seeding and cubing the cucumber, and cook the others separately, as each vegetable needs slightly different timing, until barely done. Mix the vegetables (except the beets) in fresh-made mayonnaise and lots of snipped fresh herbs. Chill. Arrange the vegetables on a cold platter and surround with the beets, which have been separately dressed in mayonnaise. Garnish with finely chopped chives and thin slices of red radish.

BLUEBERRY CRUMBLE*

SERVES 8

4 cups crushed blueberries
2 cups sugar
juice of 1 lemon
½ stick butter
1½ cups flour
pinch of salt
½ pint heavy cream, lightly whipped and flavored with sugar to taste
  and ½ teaspoon vanilla extract

Preheat oven to 350° F.

Sprinkle the blueberries with half the sugar and add the lemon juice; stir well. Place in a buttered baking dish. Blend together the ½ stick butter and the remaining ingredients. Spread this mixture over the blueberries and bake for about 40 minutes.

* Adapted from Yankee Magazine, "Favorite New England Recipes," by Sara B. Stamm. Yankee Inc., Dublin, New Hampshire, 1971.

TEA

The pleasant custom of tea breaks the long afternoon. It gives us a gentle nudge toward the rest of the day, bracing as a winter day ends, soothing at the peak of a summer afternoon. The very aroma of tea is a joy and so many delicate blends are available to us that I think it is good to keep four or five on hand, and vary them to suit your whim. At the moment I find in my cupboard oolong, so haunting and smoky; jasmine, light and loved by the Chinese; Lapsang souchong, whose taste suggests, ever so faintly, peaches; orange pekoe, very well known indeed, but of great excellence; and wonderful, strengthening Earl Grey.

Good tea is not hard to prepare. Bring fresh cold water (the better the water the better the tea; pure spring water is ideal) to a rapidly rolling boil. Rinse a porcelain or earthenware teapot with boiling water, then dry it. Spoon in the tea leaves, 5 teaspoons per quart of boiling water, allow to steep for a few minutes and pour. Extra boiling water should be placed on the tray to refresh the pot when the tea becomes too strong.

The finest teas, all of those mentioned above and many more, are provided by good merchants in tea bags as well as loose. Despite popular prejudice, the finicky professionals say that there is nothing wrong with tea bags, only with those who misuse them. If the simple rules are observed, you can make perfect tea this way. (Substitute one tea bag for one teaspoon of tea.) Just don't let the tag hang out to annoy perfectionists; remove it.

A hot cup of tea alone at four is strengthening; tea for two has made history and a middling or large tea party is just as much fun as a cocktail party. Men love them. In Boston, a bit of heated rum is often added for the gentlemen to the cup that warms; in New York, or elsewhere, one may indicate that, if wanted, a stronger drink is nearby for later.

But let us think of a tea party, large or small. It seems to me a time for restful subtle flavors, small bits that are rich but subdued. It is my feeling that the foods that are served should complement the beverage.

First choice of all, thinly sliced bread—white, orange, nut or oatmeal—the finest that you can make or buy, spread with fresh sweet butter or cream cheese. Hot buttered toast with a pot of special jam—pale-green kiwi, blueberry or apricot, perhaps, is a glorious teatime indulgence.

Cinnamon toast is a natural with tea and it is quick to prepare if you keep a jar of the sugar and cinnamon ready. Go heavy on the cinnamon and light on the sugar. Spread the toast with butter and sprinkle with the mixture. Serve meltingly hot.

Simple sandwiches made with thin-sliced bread of various sorts are suited to a more formal tea. Here are a few good ones:

Smoked Salmon with Whipped Cream Cheese
Toasted Almonds with a little Cream Cheese
Walnut, Pecan or Filbert Butter, Whipped in the Blender or Food Processor
Cucumber Sandwiches
Mushroom Sandwiches
Chicken Forcemeat with a little Cress or Lettuce
Guava Jelly with Cream Cheese
Ginger Marmalade with Cream Cheese

A very attractive way to serve the sandwiches is to arrange them in a scooped-out loaf of bread. This shell will also keep the sandwiches moist. Using a long loaf of good sandwich bread, slice off the top lengthwise. Then carefully cut out the inside of the loaf, leaving a shell ½ inch thick. Make thin sandwiches of the bread and slice them once to form triangles. Return the sandwiches carefully to the bread shell, cover with the top of the loaf and a moistened towel and refrigerate until ready to serve. Very handsome on a silver platter.

In addition to the traditional tea sandwiches, include a few sweet treats and choose among these few nourishing tidbits:

Black Walnut Lace Cookies (see Index)
Chocolate Cookies
Sugar Cookies
Jam Cookies
Perferitos (see Index)
Tiny Rich Brownies
Date Bars
Caramel Nuggets
A Fine Chocolate or Spice Cake or a Chocolate or Ginger Roll

With these last, forks should be provided. And, for a great tea party in the spring, fresh strawberries with thick clotted cream and sugar are *de rigueur*.

CHICKEN FORCEMEAT

breasts of 1 chicken
2 slices onion
1 small stalk celery, sliced
½ teaspoon thyme
1 bay leaf
salt and white pepper to taste
3 tablespoons butter
a few fresh tarragon leaves, or ½ teaspoon dried
2–3 tablespoons mayonnaise

Simmer the breasts of chicken with the next 5 ingredients in water to cover until the meat is tender—about 15 minutes. Cool, remove from the water, skin and bone the chicken breasts. Cut up and purée in the food processor with the butter and tarragon until smooth. When ready to use, add mayonnaise to give forcemeat the proper spreading consistency.

CHOCOLATE COOKIES

3 DOZEN COOKIES

This is the recipe of the Women's Industrial Union in Boston—top, top as far as I am concerned. The cookies are rich, lace-thin and a bit chewy.

¼ pound butter (1 stick)
2 squares unsweetened chocolate
1 egg, lightly beaten
¼ teaspoon salt
½ teaspoon vanilla extract
½ teaspoon baking powder
½ cup flour
1½ cups sugar

Preheat oven to 325° F.

Melt the butter and chocolate in the top of a double boiler and combine with the egg, then the other ingredients. Drop by scant teaspoonfuls on greased cookie sheets. (The finished cookies will be 3–4 inches in diameter, so space them accordingly.) Bake for about 12 minutes, watching carefully. Allow to become nearly cool before removing from the cookie sheets with a spatula. They are a little tricky at first but not at all hard after you get the hang of them, and very effective.

SUGAR COOKIES

5–6 DOZEN COOKIES

¼ pound butter (1 stick)
1 cup sugar
1 egg, well beaten
2 cups flour
½ teaspoon baking powder
1 teaspoon powdered ginger
1 tablespoon cream, either sweet or sour
sugar for topping
finely chopped nuts (optional)

Preheat oven to 400° F.

Cream together the butter and sugar, stir in the egg and sift in the flour mixed with the baking powder and ginger. Add the cream and work to a smooth ball, using your fingertips if it is easier. Chill the dough briefly in the refrigerator, then roll it out fairly thin and cut with a cookie cutter. Sprinkle each cookie with sugar and, if you wish, finely chopped nuts and bake for 4 or 5 minutes on a greased or Teflon cookie sheet. Remove the cookies from the sheet, cool and store in a cookie jar.

JAM COOKIES

½ pound sweet whipped butter (2 sticks)
½ cup sugar
3 hard-boiled egg yolks, mashed
about 2 cups flour

Preheat oven to 350° F.

Soften butter, then blend with sugar and egg yolks; add flour slowly to make a soft dough. Roll into balls about the size of walnuts, flatten slightly and make indentation in center. Bake 15–20 minutes; they should be very pale (not brown).

When cool, fill with blackberry, apricot, Damson plum, or any other jam you choose.

TINY RICH BROWNIES

ABOUT 4 DOZEN COOKIES

4 ounces bitter chocolate
5½ ounces butter
2 eggs, beaten
2 cups sugar
1 cup unsifted flour
½ teaspoon salt
2 teaspoons vanilla extract
½ cup coarsely broken nut meats

Preheat oven to 375° F.

Melt the chocolate and butter together in the top of a double boiler, then mix with the beaten eggs and add the other ingredients. Bake in a buttered 9 × 9-inch pan for 25 minutes. Cool and cut into small squares.

DATE BARS

This was the recipe of my mother, and I still think these are the most delicious small cakes to pass for tea, with fruits or ices, or to put in picnic baskets.

1 cup sugar
3 egg yolks, lightly beaten
1 8-ounce package dates
¼ cup sour cream
1 teaspoon vanilla extract
1 cup flour
1 teaspoon baking powder
pinch salt
3 egg whites, well beaten
confectioners' sugar

Preheat oven to 350° F.

Mix the sugar and egg yolks; add the next ingredients, the egg whites last. Bake in a shallow 8 × 8-inch pan for 30 minutes. Cut while still warm into bars and roll in confectioners' sugar.

CARAMEL NUGGETS

Rich and wickedly tempting.

1 cup raisins
1 cup walnuts
1 cup butter (2 sticks), at room temperature
1 cup firmly packed light brown sugar
2 teaspoons vanilla extract
2 cups flour
1 teaspoon salt

Preheat oven to 350° F.

Chop the raisins and walnuts and set aside. Cream together the butter, brown sugar and vanilla extract until light. Sift together the flour and salt and add to the creamed mixture, blending well. Stir in the raisins and nuts and spread in a greased 13 × 9-inch pan.

Bake on the middle level of the oven for 20–25 minutes. Do not overbake. Cool in the pan set on a rack, then cut into small squares. If you wish, frost with the following icing:

BROWN BUTTER ICING

¼ pound butter (1 stick)
3 cups sifted confectioners' sugar
2 tablespoons milk
2 teaspoons vanilla extract

Stir butter over medium heat until light brown. Cool slightly. Add the sugar, milk and vanilla extract and beat until smooth.

CHOCOLATE LEAVES

These make an enchanting addition to the tea tray. Their disappearance is likely to be complete.

¼ pound dark sweet chocolate
1 tablespoon liqueur
2 tablespoons butter
small fresh leaves (we used the prettily serrated leaves of meadow rue)

Melt the chocolate and the liqueur in a small double boiler. Whisk in the butter.

Wash and dry the leaves. Draw them through the chocolate mixture to coat *only the underside of the leaf* well. Place in a curved utensil (a ring mold is ideal) and refrigerate until cold and set; it will then be easy to peel the leaf from the chocolate. The lovely design of the veined leaf will be perfectly reproduced in chocolate. Arrange the chocolate leaves on a plain porcelain or silver plate and serve.

CHOCOLATE DIPPED STRAWBERRIES

Using the same recipe, dip perfect ripe strawberries in the chocolate mixture. Arrange, stem end down, on a plate so the berries will be half coated by the chocolate. Make chocolate strawberry leaves to serve with the fruit. Refrigerate until the chocolate is firm.

Chocolate violet leaves are poetic served with candied violets and, at Christmas, try chocolate holly leaves with red cinnamon candy "berries."

THE
GREAT AMERICAN
COCKTAIL
PARTY

The large cocktail party is one of New York's most exhilarating activities, popular primarily because New Yorkers are inclined to be very sociable or they wouldn't choose to live in this large exciting city. In one's acquaintance there are dozens of different groups to draw upon and a nice mingling of new friends with old can be enormous fun. People can come and go casually and it is a graceful time to invite someone whom you have met briefly and liked—a good way to begin new friendships.

Just be sure not to have too many people for cozy mingling in the space, whatever it may be, that is yours. Be sure, too, that the host or hostess can see that the new faces are properly introduced and made to feel at home. A stranger, a friend from afar, can and should feel that he adds to the glamour and *gemütlichkeit* of the evening.

Sometimes a celebratory theme can be especially nice: the viewing of some new paintings perhaps, a private anniversary, the publication of a new book or an old friend who has returned from wanderings. A lion among the lambs is always gratifying. Nice lions don't roar, they purr ever so sweetly. But see to it that *everyone* is happy. It is your party and that is your job.

Second most important is a good bar. You don't have to like bourbon to know that those who do should be served a good brand at your house. White wine is always in demand and it compliments your guests to buy a decent case. It can be modestly priced but have it to your own liking. Have a few bottles of champagne on ice for those who prefer that, or add two bottles in ice-filled buckets to the buffet table as a gala flourish. Last, but just as important, remember to have nice sparkling waters and other nonalcoholic beverages for those who prefer them.

Here is a fairly wide variety of cocktail foods (some of the sandwiches in the preceding chapter are suitable for cocktail fare, too). They should be presented in an enticing but not overpowering array, I think, on freshly and intriguingly arranged plates. There should be a few good things hot from the oven, perhaps a bubbling chafing dish. Cocktail-party food can range through a wide gamut, but at its best the array of new tastes, new aromas, the handsome display of well-thought-out baskets of crudités, sea-food plates and pretty conceits can be very tempting. As variety and new faces among the company lend the desired verve to good cocktail parties, variety and some new touches in the refreshments offered add to the fun. The French aptly call these *amuse-bouches*.

Occasionally, I encounter at parties terribly unappetizing, dreary "appe-tizers." Forget them. If time is short, a couple of excellent pâtés, a platter of cheeses at the correct temperature surrounded by delicate biscuits, good salted nuts and crisp crudités do far better. Top-quality food, good spirits among the guests and the openness of your welcome are the ingredients that must be there to make this party a memorable success.

There are a few more clues which I have gathered along the way. Take them for what they are worth, for they may apply to your mode of enter-taining.

I find that your own servant or servants lend an unsurpassable warmth to your entertaining. They are, first and always, part of your household. They like you and they care a lot about how this evening goes. They know what plates you like to use, what substitute, in a pinch, will do instead. They welcome the old guests with warmth and the new ones with courtesy and interest. Buy a pretty and becoming uniform for your maid; be sure your manservant is crisply and correctly attired. This does justice to them and to you. If you use temporary party help, stick with the same ones and soon they will begin to feel as if they belong, too.

Turn down the heat; throw open the windows and air the apartment or house well. The smell of a little cooking is tantalizing but a heavy odor of food is stultifying. Light a small fire if you have a fireplace but remember that a congregation of people will make the rooms warmer. A few greens, a few flowers, are nice, but, in general, try to avoid a studied effect.

These are some of the things that are almost staples. If you keep them on hand, you'll always be prepared when people come by for drinks on the spur of the moment.

Salted Nuts
Cheese Straws
Nut Crescents, Walnut Wafers or Other Cocktail Cookies
Pâté de Foie Gras
Olives
Crudités
Cheeses
Small Canned Button Mushrooms
Smoked Oysters

For cocktail fare for a party large or small here are a few of my favorite suggestions:

Oysters or Clams on the Half Shell Served with Buttered Brown Bread
Shrimps with Sauce Verte
Bacon-Filled Cherry Tomatoes
Fabulous Grapes
Tiny Sausages or Cheese Baked in Croissant Pastry
Sauerkraut Balls
Croques Hélène
Figs Wrapped in a Strip of Prosciutto Ham
Stilton Cheese Pear Fingers
Filet of Beef Carpaccio
Zucchini Appetizers
Small Hot Buttered Baking-Powder Biscuits Filled with Cheese or Smithfield Ham

Assorted Sandwiches:
Nut
Watercress
Smoked Salmon with Cream Cheese
Tongue
Cucumber
Bacon Strips Sprinkled with Brown Sugar
Bacon-Wrapped Chicken Livers with Pineapple, Almond-Stuffed Kumquats, Water Chestnuts or Dates
Bacon-Wrapped Bread Sticks

Eggs Stuffed with:
Mushrooms
Chopped Olives
Watercress
Ham
Or topped with a tiny bit of pale-gray caviar
A chafing dish offering Swiss Fondue, Scotch Woodcock, Braised Mushrooms or Creamed Oysters

Some of these things are more or less standard but a few recipes follow.

AN ICE JACKET FOR ICED VODKA

Place a bottle of vodka in a tall can with water reaching as high as its neck. Place in a deep freeze overnight. When ready to serve, set can in hot water until it can be slipped off. Wrap the bottle and its ice covering in a service napkin.

COFFEE PUNCH

16 CUPS

This fine punch is a good adjunct at any cocktail party and will make your party particularly pleasant for those who don't care for alcoholic beverages. Everyone else likes it too.

1¼ cups sugar
2 tablespoons cocoa
2 quarts triple-strength coffee
1 quart vanilla ice cream
½ pint heavy cream
grated orange rind

Dissolve the sugar and cocoa in a small amount of the hot coffee. Add the remaining coffee and chill overnight in the refrigerator. When ready to serve, pour the cold coffee mixture over the ice cream; add the whipped cream and grated orange rind.

THE SARATOGA COCKTAIL

Mix Saratoga, this naturally sparkling American water, with a jigger of fruit syrup, raspberry, apricot or red currant. Garnish with a spiral of lemon or orange peel and a slice of mango or a sprig of mint.

MIXED SALTED NUTS

3 POUNDS

Salted nuts, mixed or of any one kind, are superior when prepared at home and a perfect standby for before-dinner drinks or a cocktail party. My combination for mixed salted nuts is the following:

½ pound blanched raw almonds
½ pound hazelnuts
½ pound large raw cashews
½ pound midget Brazil nuts
2 tablespoons butter
2 tablespoons olive oil
½ pound large walnuts
½ pound mammoth pecans
coarse salt

Preheat the oven to 350° F.

Mix the almonds, hazelnuts, cashews and Brazil nuts with the butter and olive oil in a large roasting pan and put them on the center rack of the oven. Roast, stirring occasionally, for ½ hour. Add the walnuts and pecans. These do not need so long a cooking time as the other nuts. Salt to taste. Roast for another ½ hour, stirring occasionally, until crisp and lightly golden. The nuts will darken a little after they are removed from the oven, so do not overroast them. Drain on paper towels, cool and store in airtight jars. Serve with a sprinkling of rock salt.

Salted nuts of a single variety may be prepared in the same manner and are equally tempting.

CHEESE STRAWS

1 recipe for piecrust (see Index)
fresh-grated Parmesan cheese

Preheat oven to 450° F.

Roll piecrust ¼ inch thick and sprinkle one half with grated Parmesan cheese. Fold, press edges firmly together, fold again and roll out again to ½-inch thickness. Sprinkle with cheese and repeat the procedure twice. Cut the pastry in strips 3 inches long and ¼ inch wide. Arrange on cookie sheets and bake for 8 minutes.

NUT CRESCENTS

2–3 DOZEN

These are rich and crumbly and so good that they disappear like magic. A combination of nuts should be used—walnuts, hazelnuts, pecans, pistachios, black walnuts, whatever you have on hand. Then sprinkle poppyseeds throughout. For a cocktail party double this recipe.

1¼ cups flour
1 stick butter
1 cup chopped mixed nuts with poppyseeds
cayenne pepper
salt
dash almond extract

Preheat oven to 375° F.

Mix all ingredients together and form into small crescents using a scant teaspoon of the mixture for each and molding it around your index finger. Bake for about 20 minutes.

WALNUT WAFERS

¾ cup flour
½ cup ground walnuts
½ teaspoon baking powder
salt
½ teaspoon dry mustard
¼ pound butter (1 stick)
½ cup grated Cheddar cheese
½ cup grated Swiss cheese
1 egg, well beaten

Combine ingredients and form into a roll about 1¼ inches thick. Wrap in waxed paper and refrigerate for several hours. Preheat oven to 350° F. when needed and slice dough into thin rounds. Bake 15–20 minutes on an ungreased cookie sheet.

HOMEMADE BOURSIN

2 8-OUNCE CYLINDERS

This is a recipe of Mrs. F. William Ludington of Coral Gables, Florida, and is fresh and light and a very appetizing addition to the cheese tray.

2 (8-ounce) packages cream cheese
½ cup heavy cream
1 small clove garlic, minced
chopped parsley, basil, thyme and chives to taste
coarsely cracked black pepper

Beat all ingredients except the pepper together (the food processor does an excellent job). Chill until hard and form into 2 cylinders. Roll in coarsely cracked black pepper. This Boursin is more delicate than the more expensive store variety.

BACON-FILLED CHERRY TOMATOES

Remove stem ends of cherry tomatoes and seed and juice. Just before serving fill each with crisp crushed bacon and top with a tiny dab of sour cream.

FABULOUS GRAPES

ABOUT 24

about 24 large white seedless grapes
about 12 almonds, skinned and halved lengthwise
a few drops kirsch
¼ pound Roquefort cheese
½ pound cream cheese
½ cup finely chopped pistachios or walnuts

Stuff each grape with ½ almond. Whip together the kirsch and the cheeses, preferably in a food processor, and chill thoroughly. In the chilled palms of your hands roll the cheese around each grape to form a ball. Chill again and just before serving roll in finely chopped nuts. Arrange them to look like a bunch of grapes using watercress as leaves, unless, in summer, grape leaves are handy.

SAUERKRAUT BALLS

Mrs. F. Warrington Gillet, Jr. of Palm Beach serves these very zippy cocktail bites.

½ pound pork sausage meat, finely crumbled
¼ cup finely chopped onions
1 (14-ounce) can sauerkraut, drained and chopped*
2 tablespoons bread crumbs
3 ounces cream cheese
2 tablespoons chopped parsley
1 teaspoon prepared mustard
¼ teaspoon garlic salt
⅛ teaspoon pepper
¼ cup flour
1 egg, well beaten
¼ cup milk
¾ cup bread crumbs
sufficient oil for cooking

Cook the sausage and onions until lightly browned. Drain. Add the sauerkraut and 2 tablespoons bread crumbs. Combine cream cheese, parsley, mustard, garlic salt and pepper. Stir into meat mixture and chill.

Shape mixture into small balls and coat with flour. Combine egg and milk. Roll floured balls in egg mixture and then in ¾ cup bread crumbs. Fry in hot oil until lightly browned, about 3–5 minutes. These may be made ahead and warmed in oven before serving.

* Drain sauerkraut a day ahead if possible.

CROQUES HÉLÈNE

Recipe of Miss Helen Cutting of Park Avenue and Greenwich, Connecticut. Always popular and easy to keep on hand, these can be prepared in a large quantity and frozen.

1 loaf Pepperidge Farm white bread, sandwich thickness
4 ounces Roquefort cheese spread
1 pound bacon, cut lengthwise once and twice across

Preheat oven to 350° F.

Roll the bread slices to flatten. Trim crusts and spread with Roquefort cheese spread. Cut slices lengthwise into three strips. Roll each strip and surround firmly with one of the small strips of bacon. Secure with a toothpick. Bake about 20 minutes until bacon crisps.

FILLET OF BEEF CARPACCIO

40 PIECES

8 slices dark pumpernickel bread
sweet butter
½ pound fillet of beef, sliced raw
2 cans flat anchovies
capers
parsley

The day of the party have your butcher cut ½ pound of lean fillet of beef into thin slices and wrap tightly.

Spread pumpernickel with sweet butter; trim the crusts if you like. Cut each slice into 5 strips. Cut a slice, or a fold, of the rosy raw beef to fit each strip of bread. Arrange on the buttered bread strips, lay half an anchovy fillet on top and serve chilled, sprinkled with capers and chopped parsley.

ZUCCHINI APPETIZERS

Another new, light hors d'oeuvre from Helen Cutting.

3 cups grated zucchini (4 small)
1 cup biscuit mix
½ cup chopped onion
½ cup freshly grated Parmesan cheese
2 tablespoons chopped parsley
½ teaspoon salt
½ teaspoon seasoned salt
½ teaspoon oregano
dash pepper
1 clove garlic, mashed
½ cup vegetable oil
4 eggs

Preheat oven to 350° F.

Mix all ingredients thoroughly and spread in a buttered 13 × 9-inch pan. Bake 25 minutes. Cut into 2″ by 1″ pieces. Serve warm.

SANDWICHES

Thin sandwiches are easy to make, neat to serve and neat to eat. They can be prepared 3 or 4 hours ahead of time—not longer, or they may become tired. Use Melba-thin bread and butter it carefully. (The butter will harden when the sandwiches are chilled, serving as a coating to keep the bread from becoming soggy.) Fill the sandwiches generously and trim off the crusts with a sharp knife. Pack the sandwiches in a damp towel and store in the refrigerator until needed. Then cut into small fingers, squares or triangles, arrange on sandwich plates, garnish and serve for tea or cocktails. Here are some interesting spreads. (If you do not have time to make the sandwiches, these spreads can be whipped up in a minute in the food processor and served with crackers.)

NUT SANDWICHES

ABOUT 1½ CUPS FILLING

Mix 1 (8-ounce) package of cream cheese and ½ stick of butter with a generous quantity of nuts—blanched almonds, pistachio nuts and hazelnuts make an excellent combination. Add a small slice of onion, salt and a dash of cayenne. Whirl in the processor. Add 1 center stalk of celery, diced fine.

WATERCRESS SANDWICH SPREAD

ABOUT 1½ CUPS FILLING

Into the food processor put 1 (8-ounce) package cream cheese, ½ bunch watercress which has been washed and squeezed dry, 1 scallion, sliced, ½ bottle horseradish, which has been drained in a fine strainer and squeezed dry, and a few grinds of white pepper. Whirl until the watercress is thoroughly minced. Chill before spreadings.

SMOKED SALMON AND CREAM CHEESE SANDWICHES

ABOUT 28 SANDWICHES

In the processor beat together 1 (8-ounce) package cream cheese, 2 big dollops of cottage cheese, a dash of lemon juice, about a tablespoon of capers and finely cut chives. Spread on whole-wheat Melba-thin bread; top with thin slices of smoked salmon, ¼ pound should serve; add a grind of black pepper and top with another slice of bread spread with the cheese mixture. Cut off the crusts and store the sandwiches until needed, when they may be cut into small squares or triangles.

BACON-WRAPPED BREAD STICKS

bacon strips
1 package small Italian bread sticks
brown sugar

Preheat oven to 375° F.

Cut bacon strips in half. Wrap ½ strip bacon diagonally around each bread stick, pressing bacon firmly to the bread stick. Arrange in a shallow pan and sprinkle with brown sugar. Bake until the bacon is crisp. Drain on paper towels and serve while still warm.

STUFFED EGGS

24 STUFFED HALVES

Small eggs or pullet's eggs make more manageable bites for cocktail fare than large ones. Halved and standing upright, they look very fetching too.

To cook the eggs so that they are easy to peel, puncture the large end of each egg with a thumb tack, put the eggs in cold water to which a few tablespoons of vinegar have been added; bring slowly to the boiling point and simmer the eggs for 10–12 minutes. Drain and plunge the eggs into cold water, then refrigerate for an hour or so before peeling them.

12 hard-boiled pullet eggs
small cubes of ham, cooked mushrooms, bits of olive or watercress
5 tablespoons soft butter
3 tablespoons mayonnaise
1 teaspoon dry mustard
a few dashes of Worcestershire sauce
salt and white pepper to taste
chopped herbs, capers or anchovies for garnish, or smoked salmon and
    dill sprigs

Divide the eggs in half widthwise. Trim the bottoms so they will stand straight and remove the yolks. Arrange the eggs on a platter and add a few cubes of ham, mushrooms, olives or watercress to each egg cavity. Purée the egg yolks in a food processor or blender with the other ingredients. Spoon the mixture into a pastry bag fitted with a large star tube and fill the egg whites with the mixture, producing a spiral effect. Garnish with a bit of parsley, dill or another herb, or with capers or anchovies.

A small strip of smoked salmon curled to resemble a rosebud and garnished with one tiny sprig of dill is a delicious and extremely pretty garnish.

STUFFED EGGS WITH CAVIAR

Proceed as for Stuffed Eggs, omitting from the egg yolk filling the mustard and Worcestershire sauce. Add a little lemon juice instead to the mixture. Place a small coffee spoon of caviar, black or red, on top of each egg.

ROMANTIC
DINNERS

These slight and elegant repasts are planned for occasions that are small but special, for two dining together quietly, or sometimes for four people, an anniversary perhaps, a little celebration with dishes that can be prepared in advance or quickly produced in just the last minutes. This is the time to enjoy a little caviar, the fine wine that has been waiting for a great moment of appreciation and the niceties that one saves for small, loving occasions. They do not require anyone to serve them and, in keeping with the intimate atmosphere, you would probably wish to serve this meal yourself.

MENU I

FOR 2

with cocktails:
Oysters on the Half Shell, Lemon Halves, Sauce Mignonette
Rolled Toast

Médaillons of Veal à la Crème with Foie Gras
New Potatoes with Dill
Cucumbers Hollandaise

Oranges Orientales
Chocolate Truffles

A white Burgundy

LEMON HALVES

To prevent their juice from squirting in your eye when you are about to feast on a fine plate of oysters, or at any other time when lemons are needed, lemon halves should be wrapped in tulle and tied neatly with white kitchen string. Yellow or white tulle may be used. A sprig of parsley is decorative tied into the knot.

SAUCE MIGNONETTE

ABOUT ¼ CUP

1 teaspoon wine vinegar
1 teaspoon lemon juice
¼ cup best olive oil
2 teaspoons chopped capers
1 teaspoon chopped shallots
salt
freshly ground white pepper

Slowly beat the wine vinegar and lemon juice into the olive oil. Add the remaining ingredients and stir well.

ROLLED TOAST

SERVES 4

From *Entertaining Is an Art*, published by the Art Museum Council, Los Angeles County Museum of Art.

Freeze a loaf of fine-grained sandwich bread and slice it wafer-thin. Remove crusts and brush lightly with melted butter. Roll on the diagonal. Toast in a 275° F. oven, turning until crisp and brown on all sides.

MÉDAILLONS OF VEAL À LA CRÈME
WITH FOIE GRAS

SERVES 2

4 escalopes of veal cut in small rounded shapes
2 tablespoons sweet butter
2 slices of canned foie gras
¼ pound mushrooms, stems cut and sliced, caps whole
1 cup Sauce Suprême (recipe follows)
1 truffle, sliced

Brown the escalopes of veal in hot butter. Sandwich 2 slices together with slices of foie gras. Place on an ovenproof serving dish and surround with mushrooms cooked in the same pan. This may be done several hours ahead of time and stored in the refrigerator. Before serving pour the sauce over the *médaillons*, place a slice of truffle on each and glaze quickly under the broiler.

SAUCE SUPRÊME

ABOUT 1 CUP

In French cookery, this sauce is termed a "compound sauce" as it contains two major ingredients, a velouté sauce and fresh cream.
    First the velouté:

2 tablespoons butter
2 tablespoons flour
1 cup chicken stock
½ cup heavy cream

In a heavy-bottomed saucepan, melt the butter over low heat. Add the flour and stir together for 2 or 3 minutes (to eliminate the raw flour taste). Add the chicken stock, stirring or whisking constantly. Cook over low heat, stirring occasionally for about 15 minutes until the sauce has reduced and thickened.

To create the Sauce Suprême add the fresh cream. Stir or whisk thoroughly but do not let the sauce come to the boil. Just heat it through thoroughly. Serve.

CUCUMBERS HOLLANDAISE

SERVES 2

Unusually good!

2 seedless cucumbers, unpeeled
1 tablespoon butter
Hollandaise Sauce (see Index)

Cut cucumbers crosswise into 1½-inch lengths. Quarter each piece lengthwise and trim each quarter piece into an oval, removing the center and reserving the trimmings for another use.*

In a skillet over low heat, melt the butter and sauté the cucumber, stirring for 4–5 minutes until just tender. Serve in a heated bowl masked with Hollandaise Sauce. The deep-green, white, and yellow of the dish are very appetizing.

ORANGES ORIENTALES

SERVES 2

3 large navel oranges
1 cup water
½ cup sugar

Peel the skin from the oranges in very thin strips and cut the strips into juliennes of long thin sticks as fine as possible. In a saucepan bring the water and sugar to a boil, add the orange slivers and simmer over low heat for 15 minutes. Chill. Meantime peel the oranges, cutting away all the

---

* *Ideally, cucumber soup.*

white pith. Over a bowl, to catch the juice, cut out the sections of orange between the membranes. Arrange the orange sections on a chilled compote in an overlapping circle to resemble a rose, and spoon the candied rinds into the center of the ring. Chill.

CHOCOLATE TRUFFLES

3 DOZEN

9 ounces semisweet chocolate
1 cup heavy cream
¼ cup sweet butter (½ stick)
3 tablespoons sugar
dash Crème de Cacao
¼ cup cocoa
⅛ cup powdered instant coffee

Cut the chocolate into ½-inch pieces and melt over warm water in the top of a double boiler.

Combine the cream, butter and sugar in a heavy medium-sized saucepan and bring to a boil over medium heat, stirring. When mixture boils remove it from the heat and gently stir in the melted chocolate. Add the liqueur. Set in a pan of ice water and whip until the mixture thickens. When the mixture becomes thick and holds its shape, spoon into a pastry bag with a medium tip and pipe bite size balls onto waxed paper. Refrigerate until set. (Truffles can be refrigerated up to 2 weeks.) To serve, mix cocoa and coffee powder and roll truffles in mixture.

Truffles can also be formed using 2 teaspoons to mold mixture.

MENU II
FOR 4

with cocktails:
Prosciutto with Figs
Lemon Pepper Toast

Bay Scallops Fines Herbes
Spinach and Cheese Soufflé

Fresh Raspberries, Powdered Sugar, Crème Fraîche
Date Bars (see Index)
Irish Coffee

A Rhine or Moselle Wine

PROSCIUTTO WITH FIGS

SERVES 4

8 fresh figs
1 bunch watercress
olive oil
lemon juice
8 slices prosciutto ham
1 lime

Cut the figs in half vertically. Clean and remove large stems of the watercress and toss it in olive oil and lemon juice. Arrange a bed of watercress on 4 individual plates, place ham on the cress, place figs on each slice of ham and garnish the figs with a thin slice of lime.

LEMON PEPPER TOAST

Preheat oven to 300° F.

Cut rounds of bread and spread softened sweet butter on both sides. Sprinkle both sides liberally with lemon pepper and toast in oven until golden. Lemon pepper, a pungent mixture of dried lemon peel and black pepper, is available on the spice shelf in your market.

BAY SCALLOPS FINES HERBES

SERVES 4

A perfect light meal, bay scallops should be cooked at the last minute before serving. The whole preparation takes only 3–4 minutes.

2 pounds bay scallops
bread crumbs
finely minced herbs: dill, parsley, thyme, chives or a combination
6 tablespoons sweet butter
salt and pepper to taste
zest of 1 lemon
parsley and lemon halves for garnish

Dry the scallops in paper toweling to remove all moisture. On a big bread board roll the scallops in the bread crumbs and herbs. Sauté them in bubbling sweet butter in a large skillet, so that they will brown very quickly, until just golden. The interior of these small, tender mollusks should be barely cooked. Season to taste with a little salt and pepper and the lemon zest and serve quickly on a very hot platter garnished with parsley and lemon halves. The secret of divine scallops is in the very brief, quick cooking. La Folie in New York does them just this way.

SPINACH AND CHEESE SOUFFLÉ

1 package frozen creamed spinach
1 tablespoon butter
1 tablespoon flour
½ cup milk
2 tablespoons grated Cheddar cheese
a pinch of salt
3 eggs, separated, whites beaten until stiff

About an hour before you wish to bake it, remove the spinach from its container and place in a small buttered soufflé dish to thaw.

When ready to prepare the soufflé, preheat the oven to 400° F. Melt the butter over low heat, add the flour, the milk and the cheese and stir in the salt and egg yolks, and fold in the stiffly beaten whites. Drain the spinach mixture, level it in the dish and spoon the cheese mixture over it. Place in the oven. Cook for 5 minutes at 400° and then reduce the heat to 375°. Cook for 25 minutes longer and serve at once.

CRÈME FRAÎCHE

1 CUP

½ pint heavy cream
1 teaspoon buttermilk

In a small bowl add the heavy cream to the buttermilk. Stir well, cover and leave in a warm place overnight. The cream will come to the lovely consistency of that in Paris. Sweeten if desired.

MENU III

with cocktails:
Vodka or Champagne
Caviar and Hot Buttered Toast

Clams Casino
Hot French Bread

Roast Long Island Duckling, Sauce Bigarade
Wild Rice
Parsnip Soufflé

Watercress Salad
Frangipan Tart

Coffee
Candied Ginger

with the clams:
Champagne, if it is open from cocktails, or, if not,
a Rhine wine

Serve a good bottle of red Bordeaux with the duckling

CAVIAR

Caviar, the great moment (and getting rarer all the time), deserves the most painstaking service. At the present time the price of Beluga is well up in the three figures—that escalating sum for a 14-ounce tin. And still, I must add, there are plenty of customers for this subtle gastronomic joy. I feel that its consumption is now to be treated as a ritual of the senses. Serve it with icy vodka in the lusty tradition of feudal Russian days when the serfs brought it to the heedless Russian aristocracy in chilled buckets. Or serve it with the finest vintage of champagne, dry, chilled, balanced. Thus, the two will compliment each other in sublime perfection and every pale Russian oval will be married to the gentle sparkle of France's most festive wine.

The caviar, thoroughly chilled, should be presented on crushed ice in a silver or crystal bowl. Some experts feel that there should be no accompaniment other than hot buttered toast wrapped in a napkin to keep it hot. However, many prefer some embellishment, and these little dishes are pretty and add to the attractiveness of the presentation. You may want to serve, in small dishes, sour cream, finely minced mild onion, chopped hard-boiled egg whites and yolks, and add halves of lemon tied in tulle. ·

CLAMS CASINO

SERVES 4

24 littleneck clams
½ cup dry white wine
¼ cup sweet butter (½ stick)
2 tablespoons finely chopped parsley
2 tablespoons finely chopped shallots
1 small clove garlic, mashed
freshly ground pepper

Rinse the clams and put them in a saucepan. Add the wine and half the butter, the parsley, shallots, garlic and pepper. Cover closely and steam for 4 or 5 minutes until the clams open. Remove them with a slotted spoon; break off the shallow half of the shell and discard. Arrange the clams in the deeper shells on hot plates (snail plates if you have them; if not, in rock salt on soup plates). Cook down the liquid until it is reduced by half. Gradually add the remaining butter, tilting the pan so that you can stir rapidly with a wire whisk. The sauce should be creamy and slightly thickened. Spoon the sauce over the clams and serve.

ROAST LONG ISLAND DUCKLING WITH SAUCE BIGARADE

This is a recipe of Baroness Serge Korff of New York and Wainscott, Long Island, a clever cook and my very dear friend. A fine crisp duck is one of her specialties.

The Pekin duck is the variety of the bird which Long Island calls its own. It has a lot of fat between the meat and the skin and must be roasted slowly and long to get rid of this fat and to produce a crisp-skinned, juicy bird. There is also an interesting variation available occasionally out there called, simply, half-wild duck. This is the product of interbreeding between the passing wild duck and the local Pekin. They are flavorful, less fat but also tougher, so that they too, when available, need long, slow cooking.

1 fresh-killed duck, 5–6 pounds
salt and pepper
2 navel oranges, peeled, skinned and sliced thin
Sauce Bigarade (recipe follows)

Preheat oven to 400° F.

Rub the bird inside and out with salt and pepper; prick the skin all over with a fork; skewer the opening of the cavity and tie the legs together with kitchen string. Roast it, breast down, on a rack in the center of the oven with a pan placed beneath to catch the drippings, for 20 minutes.

Reduce oven heat to 325° F.; turn the bird on its back and continue roasting for another hour or longer, until the crisp skin clings to the meat with no fat between them. Serve with sliced oranges over the duck and Sauce Bigarade.

SAUCE BIGARADE

duck drippings
1 cup chicken broth
⅛ cup each sugar, water and currant vinegar
salt and pepper
2 tablespoons currant jelly
juice and rind of 2 oranges
½ teaspoon lemon juice
½ cup cognac

When the duck is nearly done, remove the pan that has caught the drippings as it cooked, replacing it with another. Skim excess fat from the pan and stir the chicken broth into the pan to get out all the duck juices. Pour into a heavy-bottomed saucepan and cook slowly, skimming the surface as needed. Meanwhile put the sugar and water into a small saucepan and cook over medium heat until water evaporates and syrup caramelizes to a light brown. Add currant vinegar, salt and pepper and cook until caramel is dissolved.

Add the currant jelly, orange and lemon juice, and the orange rind, which has been cut into julienne strips; blend and add to the duck stock. Stir in the cognac. If necessary, reduce a little more. Pour over duck.

WILD RICE

SERVES 4

A new and perfect technique for preparing wild rice

1 cup uncooked wild rice
boiling water
salt and butter to taste

Place raw rice in a large strainer and wash under cold running water until water runs clear. Place rice in a heavy bowl or pot. Cover with boiling water and allow to stand until water cools, about 30–45 minutes. Repeat the procedure a second time.

Three "openings" are necessary to cause wild rice to blossom fully into attractive, fluffy flowerets.

Thirty minutes before serving time, cover the drained rice with salted boiling water. At the end of 30 minutes, the rice should be fully opened. Drain in a strainer or collander; keep warm. Before serving, add salt to taste and stir in pieces of butter.

PARSNIP SOUFFLÉ I

SERVES 4

A light way to serve this delicate and sometimes neglected winter vegetable.

1 tablespoon butter
1 cup mashed seasoned parsnips
3 egg yolks, lightly beaten
4 egg whites, beaten until they form soft peaks
3 tablespoons thinly sliced Brazil nuts

Preheat the oven to 375° F.

Mix the butter into the parsnips, then the egg yolks. Fold in the egg whites and turn the mixture into a buttered soufflé dish. Sprinkle the soufflé with the nuts and bake for 25–30 minutes until puffed and golden. Serve immediately.

FRANGIPAN TART

A fascinating cookbook, *La Cuisine de Monsieur Momo*, was published in Paris in 1930. It was written by Maurice Joyant, who was the lifelong friend of Henri de Toulouse-Lautrec, his fellow student at the Lycée, his editor and art dealer, fellow cook and reveler. The book describes dishes invented, transformed and prepared by them for their friends. A fascinating glimpse into the bohemian life of the Belle Epoque. The recipes are simple but refined and among the most original and successful served in my dining room. Try this adaptation of their "Tarte Frangipane" and see for yourself how splendid it really is.

FRANGIPAN TART OR TARTLETS

Line a 9-inch flan ring with pastry. Chill in the freezer for an hour. Preheat oven to 350° F. Fill pastry shell with the frangipan filling and decorate with halved almonds. Bake on the lowest rack until golden brown, about an hour. Brush tart while still hot with apricot glaze and serve warm.

FRANGIPAN FILLING

1 cup almond paste
1½ sticks sweet butter, softened
3 eggs, beaten
2 tablespoons orange flower water
1 teaspoon grated lemon rind
3 teaspoons flour
apricot jam

Combine all ingredients except jam, first breaking the almond paste into small pieces, in the blender or food processor and blend to a smooth texture. Melt apricot jam and when warm and thin spread over the tarts.

MENU IV

This is for love in a garret, such a menu as Mimi and Rodolfo or Lara and Dr. Zhivago might have enjoyed.

Watercress Soup with Whipped Cream
Buttered Melba Toast with Sesame Seeds

Frugal Pie
Celery Rémoulade and Lettuce Salad

Soufflé Vanille with Whipped Cream

with coffee:
Peppermints

Serve Chianti or a good Spanish Rioja

WATERCRESS SOUP

SERVES 4

This lovely bright-green soup, as refreshing to look at as it is to taste, may be served either hot or chilled.

1 small onion, sliced
1 small potato, sliced
2 tablespoons butter
½ cup water
leaves of 1 bunch watercress
1 sprig parsley
1 sprig dill
2 cups chicken broth
1 cup heavy cream
salt and pepper to taste
1 egg or 2 egg yolks

Cook the onion and potato slowly in butter until a little soft, add about ½ cup water to cover and cook until very soft. Put in the blender, chop the greens (reserving 1 small sprig watercress) and add them, the chicken broth, ⅔ the cream, the salt and the pepper. Stir in the egg or egg yolks. Purée until light and frothy. Serve garnished with the remaining cream, whipped and salted, and the reserved watercress.

FRUGAL PIE

SERVES 2

So good that it seems no hardship to be poor.

1 medium onion
butter or bacon drippings
1 pound hamburger meat
1 tablespoon flour
1 cup beef bouillon
herbs, thyme or a bay leaf
salt and pepper
Kitchen Bouquet
1 cup carrots cut in olive shapes
1 cup sliced mushrooms
1 tablespoon butter
1½ cups mashed potatoes
milk for glaze

Preheat oven to 425° F.

Dice the onion and brown it gently in the fat. Remove it and crush and brown the meat in the same pan. Add the flour, bouillon, herbs and seasoning and stir until you have a nice gravy. Add the Kitchen Bouquet. Mix the onion, meat and gravy in a casserole and add the carrots and cook until just tender. Sauté the mushrooms in 1 tablespoon butter and add to casserole.

Top the pie with the mashed potatoes and glaze by brushing with a little milk. When ready to serve, place the pie in the oven until browned and bubbling hot within.

CELERY RÉMOULADE

Stored covered in the refrigerator, celery rémoulade will keep for several days and is very convenient to have. Serve it with cocktails, as a first course or to supplement a salad. It is crisp and refreshing.

1 large celery knob
1 cup (more or less) homemade mayonnaise
lemon juice
salt and freshly ground black pepper to taste
dry mustard to taste
finely cut herbs to taste

Peel the celery knob, cut it in pieces and into julienne strips or run the pieces through the food processor using the julienne blade. Blanch the celery in rapidly boiling water for only 30 seconds. Drain. Combine with homemade mayonnaise, lemon juice, salt and pepper, dry mustard and herbs.

SOUFFLÉ VANILLE
WITH WHIPPED CREAM

SERVES 2–3

The subtle simplicity of this lovely dessert is hard to equal.

1½ tablespoons butter
1 tablespoon flour
⅔ cup milk
¼ cup sugar
dash salt
3 egg yolks
½ teaspoon vanilla extract
butter
4 egg whites
confectioners' sugar
½ cup heavy cream, whipped and flavored with vanilla extract

Preheat oven to 400° F.

In a saucepan over low heat melt the butter. Mix in the flour and gradually add the milk, beating together with a wire whisk until thick. Add the sugar and salt. Remove from heat and beat in the egg yolks and vanilla extract. Cover and set aside, if you wish, until dinnertime.

Butter a 2-cup soufflé dish. Beat the egg whites until firm and glossy. Pour the yolk mixture over the whites and fold the whites into the sauce. Spoon the mixture into the soufflé dish and place in the oven. Increase the oven heat to 450° and bake for about 20 minutes. Dust the top of the soufflé with confectioners' sugar shaken through a sieve and serve with cream that has been whipped to a soft consistency and flavored with vanilla extract.

PEPPERMINTS

ABOUT 3 DOZEN SMALL PEPPERMINTS

1½ cups sugar
½ cup boiling water
5 drops peppermint oil

Dissolve the sugar in the boiling water and boil until the syrup spins a long thread. Add the peppermint and beat the mixture until creamy. Drop from the tip of a spoon onto waxed paper. Reheat the mixture if it becomes too thick.

MENU V

A Chafing-Dish Supper

with cocktails:
Sautéed Mushroom Caps
Cheese Straws (see Index)

Lump Crab Meat on Toast Points, Béchamel Sauce
Endive Salad with Thin Slivers of Brie or Camembert
Raspberry Vinaigrette Sauce

Blueberry Tarts

Champagne

A CHAFING-DISH SUPPER

SERVES 2

Arrange on the chafing-dish service tray the following:

the caps of ½ pound small mushrooms, cleaned and wiped dry
sweet butter
salt
a black-pepper grinder
a white-pepper grinder
2 lemon halves tied in tulle
a small flacon sherry
1 cup Béchamel Sauce (recipe follows)
1 pound lump crab meat in a chilled bowl
finely cut chives
parsley sprigs
a bottle of champagne

Have the toaster and bread nearby, also 2 hot shallow ramekins and 4 warm plates.

While cocktails are being mixed, light the chafing dish, melt some butter and cook the mushrooms gently in the butter, stirring and adding salt and a few grinds of black pepper, the juice of ½ lemon and some of the sherry and chives. Serve in the shallow ramekins on warm plates with cocktails.

At suppertime pour the Béchamel Sauce into the chafing dish (the mushroom juice remaining in it will be good with it) and add the crab meat. Heat thoroughly; add salt, freshly ground white pepper, the juice of ½ lemon. Open the champagne and add a dash of the bubbly to chafing dish. Cook until very hot. Arrange buttered toast points on 2 warm plates and pour crab-meat mixture over the toast points. Dust with chives and garnish with parsley. Serve with endive salad.

BÉCHAMEL SAUCE

ABOUT 1 CUP

Sauce Béchamel is the *sauce mère* of French cuisine. It is easy to make this velvety product. The simple secret is slow cooking, thorough cooking and gentle constant stirring.

2 tablespoons butter
1 teaspoon freshly grated onion
2 tablespoons flour
1 cup milk or light cream (room temperature)
salt and white pepper to taste
pinch nutmeg

Melt the butter in a saucepan over low heat. Add the grated onion and cook until soft without browning the onion. Stir in the flour to make a *roux*. Gradually add the milk or cream, stirring the mixture as you do, and cook gently, stirring the sauce until it is thick and reduced to the desired consistency. It should be cooked like this for 5 or 10 minutes so that the sauce will be thick and smooth and the flour well cooked. Add the seasonings.

ENDIVE SALAD WITH THIN SLIVERS OF BRIE OR CAMEMBERT

½ pound endive
¼ pound Brie or Camembert cheese
Raspberry Vinaigrette Sauce (recipe follows)

While preparing the chafing-dish supper have a bottle of champagne chilling in the refrigerator.

Just before supper sliver the endive and toss it in Raspberry Vinaigrette Sauce. Arrange on salad plates alternating the endive slivers with slivers of Brie or Camembert. Leave at room temperature for the cheese to soften a little.

RASPBERRY VINAIGRETTE SAUCE

ABOUT ¾ CUP

½ cup olive oil
4 tablespoons raspberry vinegar
½ teaspoon salt
¼ teaspoon ground pink peppercorns
1 tablespoon crème fraîche

Combine all ingredients. Shake well.

BLUEBERRY TARTS

Unusually good, and useful since blueberries now seem to be available almost the year round. (Makes 2 generous individual tarts or 3 less large ones.)

1 pint blueberries
1½ cups sugar
1 tablespoon plus 1 teaspoon cornstarch
2 or 3 individual tart shells
¾ cup heavy cream, whipped

Wash and pick over the blueberries. Reserving half of them, cook the other half over low heat with the sugar and cornstarch for about ½ hour. Set aside. Fill the tarts with whipped cream and chill. When ready to serve, divide the fresh berries between the tarts and pour the warmish cooked berry sauce over them. Garnish with a dollop of whipped cream and serve.

MENU VI

Smoked Salmon
Lemon Halves
Black Pepper
Whole-Grain Sweet Butter Sandwiches

Mixed Grill
Béarnaise Sauce

Ginger Jubilee Flambé

A Côte du Rhône

with coffee:
Glazed Brazil Nuts

MIXED GRILL

SERVES 4

Always popular with guests, mixed grill is a great joy for the hostess too, as it can be prepared and assembled on a platter an hour before dinner and kept warm in a low oven.

8 Jones country sausages
12 slices bacon
4 double-thick loin lamb chops
4 lamb kidneys
salt and pepper
2 large tomatoes, halved
herbed, seasoned bread crumbs
4 large mushroom caps
butter
chopped parsley

In a large skillet brown the sausage and bacon, 2 sausages and 3 strips of bacon for each serving. Drain on paper toweling and discard most of the grease from the skillet. Brown the chops and sliced kidneys quickly so that they are still pink inside. Season with salt and pepper and remove them to a large platter which can go in the oven.

Halve some fine big tomatoes which are not fully ripe, dip them in herbed, seasoned bread crumbs and sauté them very briefly in the same skillet with added butter. Sauté the mushroom caps next. Arrange the tomatoes and mushrooms around the chops, add the sausages and garnish the whole with bacon curls. Put the platter in a 150° F. oven until serving time, at the same time putting in the plates for the meal. When ready to serve, garnish the platter with parsley.

BÉARNAISE SAUCE

ABOUT 1 CUP

2 teaspoons tarragon vinegar
1 tablespoon white wine
2 teaspoons chopped tarragon
¼ pound butter (1 stick)
3 egg yolks
1 tablespoon lemon juice
salt
freshly ground black pepper
½ teaspoon meat glaze or 1 tablespoon meat juices

Combine the vinegar, wine and tarragon and cook until the liquid is reduced by half. In the top of a double boiler melt a third of the butter, add the liquid and the egg yolks and stir constantly over hot but not boiling water until slightly thickened. Add another third of the butter, stir until thickened and then add the rest of the butter, the lemon juice and the salt and pepper to taste. Add the meat glaze or a tablespoon of the juices in which you are cooking the accompanying meat. Stir until thick and keep in a warm place, stirring occasionally until needed. If the sauce should curdle or separate it can be brought back to a smooth consistency by stirring in a teaspoonful of boiling water, a small ice cube or a teaspoonful of heavy cream.

GINGER JUBILEE FLAMBÉ

SERVES 4

A chafing-dish drama.

zest of 1 orange
¾ cup ginger marmalade
2 tablespoons confectioners' sugar
1 tablespoon Curaçao
2 jiggers brandy
1½ pints vanilla ice cream

Cut thin shavings from the orange and shred them into fine julienne strips. Combine with the ginger marmalade in a chafing dish. Add the sugar, Curaçao and brandy. Ignite and pour the flaming sauce over the ice cream, which has been divided and portioned in 4 well-chilled deep dessert dishes.

GLAZED BRAZIL NUTS

1 cup light corn syrup
Brazil nuts

Heat the corn syrup to 310° F. on a candy thermometer, then cool quickly by plunging the pan in cold water. Place pan in hot water and throw in the nuts and stir to glaze them. Cool them on a cookie sheet. Break the glazed nuts apart and chill.

DINNER AT
EIGHT

"Dinner at eight," a magic catchphrase for hostess and guest, a magic number in entertaining for both the appointed hour and what many hosts and hostesses think an ideal number of guests: eight or ten so that conversation does not pall and can be revived by a fresh voice, eight or ten to create a mixture of guests with varying interests and backgrounds, divergent but congenial, at the table.

Menus written for dinner with dress and a bit of formality, these are ideal for a sit-down party. I always have place cards, and menus at each end of the table for this kind of dinner. Perhaps the service is easier for you spread out buffet style for the guests to help themselves. In that case, a soup tureen will prove invaluable. Either way, to enjoy yourself more thoroughly you will probably want to have someone serve and remove the dishes. If you choose to serve a buffet, be sure to use your very largest dinner napkins to protect best dresses from spills and have enough little tables about to take care of wineglasses safely. If you don't feel you need a servant, Menu III is as simple as possible, or you might consider omitting the first courses altogether from any of the others. The entrees are sustaining without them and since slenderness and health are more in vogue these days than overeating, they aren't essential.

Try to have your party seated promptly at 8:45 or 9:00 at the latest. Latecomers and cocktail lingerers should not spoil the timing of a good dinner with its wines, and the polite and punctual do not wish to continue the cocktail hour ad tedium. There will be plenty of time for talking and relaxing over coffee and cognac.

Usually, but not always, I have suggested cocktail accompaniments with these dinners. Otherwise, consult *The Great American Cocktail Party* chapter, which includes all sorts of possibilities.

MENU I

---

with cocktails:
Smoked Salmon on Romaine Lettuce Leaves Garnished with Capers
Herb Buttered Brown Bread

Essence of Celery Soup

Suprême de Volaille à la Crème Strasbourgeoise on Noodles
Purée of Broccoli with Broccoli Flowerets
Carrots with Mint

Jelly of Caffè Espresso with Crème Fraîche
Black Walnut Lace Cookies

White Burgundy or Champagne or Both

with coffee:
Chocolate-Dipped Strawberries

ESSENCE OF CELERY SOUP

SERVES 8

1 bunch celery
3 quarts well-seasoned chicken broth
salt
salted whipped cream

Clean and trim the celery, reserving the heart. Dice the celery and some of its leaves quite fine. Simmer in the chicken broth without a cover for 30 minutes. Pass through a fine strainer. Serve hot or cold garnishing each soup plate with a slice of celery heart and salted whipped cream.

SUPRÊME DE VOLAILLE À LA CRÈME
STRASBOURGEOISE ON NOODLES
Breast of Chicken in Cream with Foie Gras on Noodles

SERVES 8

This is chicken at its most sublime, and a very valuable recipe, as it is a dish that must be prepared in advance for the flavors to grow together. This recipe, given for 8, can be multiplied or divided with ease.

breasts of 4 chickens
1 onion, sliced
1 lemon, sliced
1 bay leaf
salt and pepper to taste

Rinse the chicken and simmer with the other ingredients in enough water to cover until done, about 15 minutes. Cool. Skin and bone the chicken, discarding the skin and bones. Divide each breast in 2 pieces. Strain, then skim the broth.

4 tablespoons butter (½ stick)
4 tablespoons flour
1 cup of the chicken broth
½ cup heavy cream
½ cup Chablis
2 ounces pâté de foie gras
heavy cream

Melt the butter over low heat, add the flour and stir for 3 minutes until cooked and perfectly smooth. A little at a time and stirring to keep the sauce smooth, add the broth, the cream and the Chablis. Last add the foie gras, blended with an equal amount of heavy cream. Taste for seasoning and set aside, refrigerated if necessary, until ready to serve.

1 pound thin noodles
salt
4 tablespoons butter
1 truffle, sliced

Boil the noodles in salted water *al dente*, drain, butter and pour on a hot platter. Arrange the chicken breasts on the noodles, pour the hot sauce over the dish, and garnish with truffle slices.

PURÉE OF BROCCOLI WITH BROCCOLI FLOWERETS

SERVES 8

2 heads broccoli
salt
about 1 stick butter
about ½ cup heavy cream
juice ½ lemon

Clean the broccoli. With a small paring knife remove the flowerets with an inch or so of their stems. Boil these rapidly in salted water until bright green and tooth-tender. Drain and set aside. Cut the tough ends from the rest of the broccoli, pare the stems and cut into pieces. Boil these rapidly in salted water until tender (they should cook longer than the flowerets). Drain and put in the food processor fitted with the steel blade. Purée, adding some butter and cream until you have a smooth, light mixture. Put the purée in a covered saucepan and set aside. At serving time reheat the two separately. Spoon the purée into a hot serving dish, arrange the flowerets in it like a bouquet, squeeze lemon juice on the dish, brush with more butter and serve.

JELLY OF CAFFÈ ESPRESSO WITH CRÈME FRAÎCHE

SERVES 8

Light but rich, I find this an excellent dinner party dessert. From Steven Connell.

3 tablespoons gelatin
¾ cup coffee liqueur
3 cups hot espresso coffee
¾ cup sugar
pinch salt
2 cups heavy cream, whipped until stiff
1 cup crème fraîche (see Index)

Soften the gelatin in the coffee liqueur and dissolve it in the hot coffee. Add the sugar and salt. Cool until syrupy; fold in the whipped cream and pour into a 1½-quart ring mold that has been rinsed out with water. Chill in the refrigerator until stiff, unmold, fill the center with crème fraîche and serve.

BLACK WALNUT LACE COOKIES

ABOUT 24 COOKIES

¼ pound butter (1 stick)
½ pound light-brown sugar
½ teaspoon vanilla extract
1 egg
1 cup old-fashioned oatmeal
½ cup coarsely chopped black walnuts

Preheat oven to 350° F.

Melt the butter and add to it the sugar and vanilla extract. Beat the egg lightly with a fork and stir into the mixture. Stir in the oatmeal and black walnuts.

Cover cookie sheets with lightly oiled aluminum foil. (The foil may be used over and over, and it is not necessary to grease it again.) Drop the dough by level teaspoonfuls far apart and cook until the cookies are spread very thin and slightly dry, about 10 minutes. To remove the cookies peel the foil away from them rather than using a spatula.

MENU II

This is a nice change for an autumn or winter party. It is built around a stuffed loin of pork and is not difficult to prepare or to serve.

with cocktails:
Stuffed Small Tomatoes
Cheese Straws (see Index)
Fabulous Grapes (see Index)

Potage Forestière

Roast Stuffed Loin of Pork with Roast Potatoes
and Stuffed Prunes
Spinach en Branche
Warm Applesauce
Crusty Rolls

Pesche Ripiene

with coffee:
Chocolate Covered Mints

A Fine Red Burgundy with This Hearty Dinner

POTAGE FORESTIÈRE
Fresh Mushroom Soup

This soup, which has a genuine woodsy taste, makes an interesting appearance with its garnish of whole mushroom caps. It can be made in 15 or 20 minutes.

4 tablespoons butter
1 onion
1 pound mushrooms
4 tablespoons flour
2 cups chicken broth
¾ teaspoon salt
3 cups whole milk
2 tablespoons sherry
whipped cream and watercress for garnish

In a good-sized pot melt the butter over a low flame. Mince the onion and cook it gently in the butter until soft. Chop the mushroom stems and add them and the flour at the same time, gradually stirring in 1 cup of the chicken broth and the salt. Cook until smooth, then remove this mixture from the stove and purée in the blender or food processor. Pour the purée back into the pot and a little at a time add the milk and the rest of the chicken broth, while stirring to keep the soup smooth. Reserve 1 whole mushroom cap for each serving. Slice the rest of the mushrooms very, very thin. Add them all to the soup and cook over low heat for 5 minutes more. The flour should be thoroughly absorbed and the mushrooms tender but not limp. Two tablespoons of good sherry is enough to add a little zest to the soup without concealing the taste of the fresh mushrooms. Garnish each plate with a mushroom, cold whipped cream and a small sprig of watercress.

ROAST STUFFED LOIN OF PORK
WITH ROAST POTATOES

1 (4–5-pound) boned loin of pork
Stuffing (recipe follows)
salt and pepper to taste
12–14 potatoes peeled and boiled in salted water
Stuffed Prunes (recipe follows)

Preheat oven to 375° F.

Lay the boned loin of pork flat and spread it with the Stuffing. Roll it up tight and tie it securely with string. Salt and pepper it. Roast for about 3 hours. Add boiled potatoes to the pan for the last ¾ hour of cooking and turn them frequently to brown well. Remove the roast and the potatoes to a hot platter; garnish with Stuffed Prunes. Add flour and water to the pan juices as well as the juices from the prune marinade to make a pan gravy. Season to taste.

STUFFING FOR THE LOIN OF PORK

ABOUT 4 CUPS

This makes a nice firm stuffing that will hold the meat together neatly.

1 pound sausage meat
1 onion, chopped
1 stalk celery, chopped
2 cups seasoned bread crumbs
1 cup chicken broth

In a large skillet break up the sausage meat to brown it and at the same time braise the vegetables a little in the melting fat. Add the bread crumbs and the broth. Stir together, cool and spread on the loin.

STUFFED PRUNES

SERVES 8–10

1 pound very large prunes
2 cups boiling water
½ cup Quetch (an eau-de-vie made from plums)
blanched whole almonds
almond paste (optional)

Put prunes in boiling water and Quetch and marinate for 24 hours or longer. Next day remove the stones with a sharp knife and insert instead an almond or some almond paste, or both. Serve warm around the roast using any extra juice to enhance the gravy. These prunes are particularly good with pork, ham or goose.

PESCHE RIPIENE
Fresh Peaches Stuffed with Macaroons

SERVES 8–10

6 firm but ripe peaches
5 stale macaroons, crushed with a rolling pin or in a blender (1 cup
  crumbs)
2 tablespoons sugar
¼ cup unsalted butter (½ stick), softened
2 egg yolks

Preheat oven to 375° F.

Blanch the peaches, 2 at a time, in boiling water for about 20 seconds. Lift them out with a slotted spoon and plunge them into cold water; peel off the skins with a small sharp knife.

Cut the peaches in half and remove the pits. Scoop enough peach pulp out of each half to make a deep space in the center.

Add the pulp to the crushed macaroons, then stir in the sugar, butter and egg yolks. Stuff the peach halves with the macaroon-pulp mixture.

Arrange the peach halves side by side in a buttered 8 × 10-inch baking dish or on an ovenproof platter and bake them for about 25 minutes until they are just tender. Baste with sugar syrup from the pan during baking. Serve hot or cold.

MENU III

Terribly easy to present, not expensive, and as good as any dinner in the book, this menu is ideal for a night when you are busy yourself and not expecting help.

with cocktails:
Plateau de Fromages
Crudités
Salted Nuts

Boeuf Bourguignonne
Rice
Buttered Asparagus Spears
Hot Herbed Bread

Poires en Croûte with Caramel Sauce

with coffee:
Jordan Almonds
Brandy
Crème de Menthe

A hearty Burgundy, either French or one of our New York or California wines.

BOEUF BOURGUIGNONNE

SERVES 10

I have never known anyone who doesn't agree that this is the very best "beef stew." Other efforts, including such extraneous matter as olives, water chestnuts, artichokes, have been made by those who like to innovate, but I don't think any one of them holds a patch to this honest dish.

This formula is worked out so that it is easy to multiply or divide: for each 5 people, 2 pounds of good beef, ¾ pound carrots, ¾ pound mushrooms, onions, etc. Here is an ample recipe for 10 which I find is the amount most often made. There will probably be a little left over. It keeps well.

4 pounds lean beef, sirloin tip, top of the round, or porterhouse tip cut in cubes
flour
salt and pepper to taste
4 tablespoons bacon fat
4 tablespoons butter
bay leaf
2 or 3 large cloves garlic, mashed
1½ pounds carrots, as young as available
1½ pounds mushrooms, cleaned and coarsely sliced
2 tablespoons butter
1 cup Burgundy
1 cup beef stock
2 packages tiny frozen creamed onions
tomato paste (optional)
parsley or chives for garnish

Let the meat come to room temperature. Mix ½ cup or more of flour with salt and pepper and coat the pieces of meat in the mixture. Sauté them, a portion at a time, in a very large frying pan in a combination of bacon fat and butter. Crumble in the bay leaf. When the pieces of meat are brown remove them to a 4-quart ovenproof casserole. Continue until all the meat is cooked. During the cooking of the last batch add the garlic (don't add it early, as burned garlic tastes awful).

Scrape the carrots and cut in large julienne sections, or leave them whole if they are tiny; boil until nearly tender in water to cover. Reserve water. Sauté mushrooms briefly in butter.

Add the wine, stock and frozen onions to the pan in which the meat was cooked and stir to form a thick, smooth sauce. If more liquid is needed, use some of the water in which the carrots were cooked. Taste for seasoning. If you like, a small amount of tomato paste may be added. Transfer the vegetables to the casserole with the beef; pour the gravy over the dish and set aside. Place in a preheated 350° F. oven an hour before serving. Garnish with finely cut parsley or chives.

POIRES EN CROÛTE WITH
CARAMEL SAUCE
The recipe of Nancy Yerby

SERVES 10

Pâté Sucré (recipe follows)
10 bosc pears
1 cup finely ground walnuts (other nuts may be used)
1 cup sugar
nutmeg to taste
cinnamon to taste
2 eggs, lightly beaten
Caramel Sauce (recipe follows)

Preheat oven to 350° F.

Peel and core the pears, leaving the pear and stem intact. Mix the ground nuts, sugar and spices; coat the pears with this mixture and stuff some of it into the cavities.

Roll out the Pâté Sucré ½ inch thick and cut into squares of about 6 inches. Envelop each pear in a square of pastry, allowing the stem to protrude and tucking the ends of the pastry into the cavities of the pears. Cut pastry leaves from the scraps of pastry and decorate the pears with these. Brush with egg to glaze and bake for 45–50 minutes until golden. Serve warm or at room temperature with Caramel Sauce.

PÂTÉ SUCRÉ

1 RECIPE

3 cups sifted all-purpose flour
3 egg yolks
3 tablespoons sugar
12 ounces butter (3 sticks)
grated rind of 1 lemon
pinch salt

Sift the flour into a mixing bowl. Make a well in the center and add the remaining ingredients.

Mix the center ingredients with the fingers of one hand or a pastry blender until blended. Work quickly with the flour. Add a small amount of ice water, if necessary, so the pastry can be gathered into a ball. This procedure can be accomplished almost instantly in a food processor fitted with the pastry blade.

Wrap the dough in waxed paper and chill for 1 hour.

CARAMEL SAUCE

ABOUT 3 CUPS

2 cups sugar
¾ cup water
pinch cream of tartar
2 cups heavy cream, heated

Cook the sugar and water together over medium heat until caramelized, stirring as you cook. Add the cream of tartar. Remove from heat and add the heated cream. Stir together and serve warm with the pears.

MENU IV

FOR 8

---

with cocktails:
Lump Crab Meat with Sauce Verte and Capers
Toasted Chive Sandwiches

Crème Bordelaise

Stuffed Breast of Veal with Mushroom Sauce
Sweet Potato Croquettes
Courgettes aux Tomates

Bombe au Cassis
Macaroons
Chocolate Leaf Cookies

Café Brûlot

With the main course serve the best bottle of red Bordeaux you have, which has, of course, been opened ahead of time and allowed to breathe in peace for ½ hour. Open a bottle of chilled champagne with the dessert.

SAUCE VERTE

---

1 CUP

1 egg
¼ teaspoon dry mustard
½ teaspoon salt
1 tablespoon lemon juice
½ cup best olive oil
½ cup vegetable oil
wash and dry the following greens and remove stems:
    handful watercress leaves
    2 branches fresh parsley
    fresh tarragon or basil leaves, if available
salt and freshly ground white pepper

Put whole egg with mustard and salt in a food processor or blender and blend for 20 seconds. Pour in lemon juice and blend again. Add oils slowly until mixture starts to thicken. Add the greens and purée until the sauce is thick. Season to taste with salt and freshly ground white pepper.

TOASTED CHIVE SANDWICHES

24 SMALL SANDWICHES

4 ounces cream cheese
1 bunch chives, finely chopped
12 slices Melba-thin white bread
4 ounces butter

Soften the cream cheese and mix in the chives. Spread on 6 slices of the bread and cover firmly with the other 6 slices. Trim the crusts. When ready to serve cut each sandwich in 4 small triangles and sauté quickly in butter on both sides. Drain on paper toweling and serve hot.

CRÈME BORDELAISE

SERVES 8

¼ pound butter (1 stick)
1 pound young carrots, cleaned and sliced
1 quart seasoned chicken stock
1 cup cooked rice
3 egg yolks
1 cup heavy cream
salt and pepper to taste
chopped leaves of mint or lemon balm

Melt the butter in a casserole, add the carrots and simmer gently until soft, stirring often so they will not stick to the pan. Pour on this the chicken stock and add the rice. Cook slowly together for 10 minutes. Purée. Heat again and thicken with the egg yolks beaten with the cream. Season to taste and serve hot in individual bowls, garnished with chopped herbs.

STUFFED BREAST OF VEAL WITH MUSHROOM SAUCE

SERVES 8

A classic French dish, as prepared by Steven Connell.

*1 (4–5 pound) breast veal, boned, trimmed and prepared for stuffing
    (a pocket will be cut in the veal by the butcher)*
1 package frozen spinach, defrosted and drained
1 cup cooked rice
¼ cup ground ham
salt and pepper to taste
flour as needed
1 cup chicken broth
1 pound mushrooms, cleaned, stemmed and sliced
½ cup heavy cream
1 jigger cognac

Mix together the spinach, rice and ham; add salt and pepper to taste; stuff into the pocket of the veal. Roll the veal tightly and tie securely with kitchen string. Pat flour over the surface of the meat and braise in the chicken broth in a covered skillet, turning occasionally, for about 1 hour until done.

Remove the veal to a hot platter and add the sliced mushrooms to the liquid in the pan. Cook while stirring to reduce the liquid to a smooth sauce. Add the heavy cream and cognac. Taste for seasoning and pour over the veal.

COURGETTES AUX TOMATES

Courgettes are, of course, zucchini. I think the French word sounds prettier, somehow.

2 pounds courgettes, sliced thin
1 pound tomatoes, just turning from green to red, sliced
¼ pound butter (1 stick)
salt to taste
1 tablespoon raspberry vinegar
1 tablespoon freshly ground pink peppercorns
1 tablespoon finely minced parsley

Sauté the courgettes and tomatoes in butter until just tender. Season with salt and raspberry vinegar and serve sprinkled with peppercorns and parsley.

SWEET POTATO CROQUETTES

SERVES 8

3 cups sweet potatoes, cooked and riced
3 tablespoons softened butter
salt, white pepper and cayenne pepper to taste
2 eggs, lightly beaten
¾ cup milk
1 cup seasoned bread crumbs
fat for deep frying

Beat together the potatoes, butter and seasonings. Chill. Shape into balls, using tablespoons. Roll quickly into cylinders, roll in the egg mixed with the milk, then the bread crumbs, chill again and deep-fry at 375° F. until golden. The croquettes may be kept warm in a low oven for ½ hour or so until serving time.

BOMBE AU CASSIS

I think this dessert is devastating—divine—delectable.

1 quart French vanilla ice cream
1 quart Cassis sherbet
1 (12-ounce) jar black currant preserve
2 jiggers crème de Cassis

Fill a 2-quart mold with the vanilla ice cream, covering the sides and leaving a hollow in the center. Fill with Cassis sherbet. Freeze until very hard and firm. Beat the black currant preserve and crème de Cassis together in a bowl. Refrigerate. At serving time unmold the bombe onto a cold serving dish, surround with the sauce and serve.

MACAROONS

ABOUT 36 COOKIES

One of my favorite of all cookies, macaroons are simple to prepare and they keep very well.

1 pound almond paste
2 cups confectioners' sugar
4 egg whites
2 teaspoons vanilla extract

Break the almond paste into small pieces and combine the ingredients in the food processor or blend them by hand. Chill the mixture, then drop small teaspoonfuls on cookie sheets lined with unglazed paper and bake for about 20 minutes in an oven preheated to 350° F. until light golden. Remove the paper to a damp dish towel for a few minutes and remove the cookies with a spatula to a wire rack. When cool, store in an airtight tin.

CHOCOLATE LEAF COOKIES

1 recipe Pâté Sucré dough (see Index)
2 ounces semisweet chocolate

Make the Pâté Sucré dough and chill it. Roll out and cut into leaf-shaped cookies. (If you don't have a leaf-shaped cookie cutter one can be formed by reshaping a star- or heart-shaped cutter. Both of these are easy to find.) Bake the cookies without the additional sprinkling of sugar. Remove them from the cookie sheets. Cool. Melt the chocolate in the top of a double boiler and with a pastry brush cover each cookie thickly with chocolate. Cool and then chill the cookies. Store in a tightly covered tin.

CAFÉ BRÛLOT

8–10 DEMITASSE CUPS

Place in a chafing dish:

Peel of 1 orange, cut in thin julienne strips
Peel of ½ lemon, cup in thin julienne strips
12 cloves
6 lumps sugar
½ cup cognac
6 cups freshly brewed coffee

Light the flame under the chafing dish and ladle the ingredients until the sugar is dissolved. Ignite the dish and add the coffee.
   Serve in demitasse cups.

MENU V

This is a nice dinner for a warm spring night.

with cocktails:
Crudités
Toasted Almond Sandwiches

Moules à la Marinière
French Bread

Sweetbreads à la Crème with Mushrooms in White Rice Ring
New Peas à la Française (see Index)

Ice Cream with Raspberry Sauce en Soufflé

with Coffee:
Crème de Menthe Frappé

A Vouvray or White Bordeaux

with dessert:
Château d'Yquem

TOASTED ALMOND SANDWICHES

24 SMALL SANDWICHES

6 slices Melba-thin white bread
butter, softened
4 ounces cream cheese, softened
3 ounces toasted salted almonds, chopped

Spread the bread with butter, then with cream cheese. Sprinkle liberally with toasted almonds, form into sandwiches and remove the crusts. Cut into small triangles and serve. These sandwiches should not be prepared very long in advance as the almonds should be crisp.

MOULES À LA MARINIÈRE

SERVES 6

A recipe of Claude Sarfati, the former owner chef of the Huntting Inn in Easthampton, Long Island. While the Sarfatis operated this inn, which was established in 1751, they added a European flavor to its menus. Seafood there on the South Fork is fresh, varied and abundant and tends more and more to be the choice of those who like the simple and the best. These plump apricot-colored mussels resting in their blue-purple shells and flecked with green herbs are as lovely to look at as they are delightful to know.

3 pounds fresh mussels
1 teaspoon minced shallots
finely minced dill, tarragon and parsley
2 glasses medium-dry white wine
sea salt
white pepper

Scrub the mussels under running cold water with your hands and, if necessary, fresh steel wool until thoroughly clean. This is not hard. Put the mussels in a large pot over a high flame with the wine and the other ingredients and simmer, covered, for 5 minutes until they open wide. They will yield their own broth. Serve steaming.

SWEETBREADS À LA CRÈME WITH
MUSHROOMS IN WHITE RICE RING

Easy to prepare, a light and festive main course for a small dinner party.

4 pairs sweetbreads
2 tablespoons chopped shallots
9 tablespoons butter
1½ cups sliced white mushrooms
3 tablespoons flour
1 cup light cream
salt and white pepper to taste
2 egg yolks
½ cup heavy cream
the juice from the mushrooms
White Rice Ring (recipe follows)
greens, parsley or watercress for garnish

The day before, blanch sweetbreads in salted water to cover, cooking them just a minute after the water boils. Drain them, transfer to a bowl, cool and weight down. Refrigerate overnight. Next day peel off the outer tissues.

Sauté the chopped shallots in 4 tablespoons of the butter, add the sweetbreads and cook gently until tender, 2–3 minutes. Sauté the mushrooms in 2 tablespoons of the butter.

Melt the remaining 3 tablespoons butter over low flame, add the flour, stirring, and gradually add the cream. Stir until thick and smooth, about 3 minutes. Season with salt and white pepper.

In a bowl beat the egg yolks until light and pale; beat in the heavy cream. Beat these slowly into the sauce. Add the juices from the mushrooms.

Arrange the sweetbreads in the center of a White Rice Ring on a heated platter, add the mushrooms to the sauce and pour over the sweetbreads. Garnish and serve.

WHITE RICE RING

6-CUP MOLD

6 cups cooked white rice (see Index)
cooking oil

Press the rice, while hot, firmly into an oiled ring mold. Unmold on a hot platter.

ICE CREAM WITH RASPBERRY SAUCE EN SOUFFLÉ

SERVES 6–8

This dessert is as pretty and as delicious as baked Alaska and very, very easy to make.

1 round layer pound cake or angel food cake
1 quart French vanilla ice cream
1 package frozen raspberries
1 jigger eau de framboise liqueur
4 egg whites
sugar to taste
candied rose petals
pink sugar

Cut a round of the cake ½ inch thick to fit the bottom of an 8-inch freezer-to-oven casserole and fit it into the dish. Spread the ice cream over the cake, making a hollow in the ice cream. Purée the raspberries in the food processor or blender and strain to remove the seeds. Add the framboise to the purée and pour the mixture into the hollowed ice cream. Place in the freezer until just before serving.

Before serving, preheat the oven to 500° F. Beat the egg whites until they form stiff peaks, beat in sugar to taste and turn lightly on top of the ice-cream casserole, making sure that the egg white meets the edges of the casserole at all points to insulate the ice cream. Place on a board and bake on the center shelf of the oven for about 3 minutes, until the meringue is puffed and slightly browned. Decorate with candied rose petals and pink sugar and serve at once.

MENU VI

Lobster Soup
Cheese Straws (see Index)

Stuffed Crown Roast of Lamb
Flageolets Fines Herbes
Aubergines Toulousiennes
Broiled Tomatoes
Red Currant Jelly

Date Pudding

Serve either a red Bordeaux or a Burgundy, as you like.

LOBSTER SOUP

SERVES 8

6 tablespoons butter
4 tablespoons flour
3 cups milk
2 cups light cream
2 cups lobster meat, diced
2 teaspoons chopped fresh tarragon
1 teaspoon salt
½ teaspoon white pepper
¼ teaspoon ground mace or nutmeg
2 jiggers dry sherry
2 egg yolks
tarragon leaves for garnish

Melt the butter over low heat and blend in the flour. Add the milk slowly, stirring constantly to make a smooth sauce. Add the other ingredients and simmer gently for 10 minutes. Serve in heated soup plates garnished with fresh tarragon leaves.

STUFFED CROWN ROAST OF LAMB

A party dish *par excellence,* this roast is composed of the choicest cut of lamb, the loin chops, and cooked only until pink and juicy. Serve it on a round platter surrounded with broiled tomatoes, garnished with paper frills, little bouquets of parsley and watercress bursting from the center of the roast. It has great *éclat.*

Have your butcher prepare a crown roast. He will use a double rack consisting of 8 chops each. Ask him to grind the meat trimmings and stuff the center of the roast. He will top each little shank with a paper frill.

1 crown roast of lamb, stuffed with ground lamb
salt and pepper
¼ cup finely chopped shallots
the ground lamb from the center of the roast
½ cup minced parsley
½ pound mushrooms, diced
dried rosemary, salt and pepper to taste
1 tablespoon grated lemon rind
watercress and parsley for garnish
10 broiled tomatoes to surround the base of the roast

Preheat oven to 350° F.

Remove the paper frills and set aside until serving time. Take the ground lamb from the center of the roast and braise it in a skillet with the minced shallots, parsley, mushrooms, seasonings and lemon rind until partially cooked. Stuff the mixture back into the middle of the roast.

Set a Pyrex bowl 4 inches or so in diameter, top down, beneath the center of the crown in the roasting pan. This will hold the ribs in a firm, upright position. The stuffing can be mounded stylishly high over the bowl, which will also serve to conduct heat evenly to the center of the roast.

Place roast, which has been seasoned with salt and pepper, in oven and baste occasionally until the meat is cooked to the desired stage of pinkness, testing frequently. This will probably take less than 1 hour.

Remove the lamb from the oven to a hot platter. Garnish with the paper frills and arrange bouquets of greens on top and grilled tomatoes around the base of the roast.

These small white beans are served frequently with roast lamb by the French. Like love and marriage the two are a truly superior combination. Dried flageolets are available in good grocery stores. If you are a gardener it's an interesting and useful crop to include among your vegetables. When they mature they can be eaten fresh or dried for winter use.

I'd like to digress here to mention my favorite seed house, J. A. Demonchaux of 827 North Kansas, Topeka, Kansas 66608, where all sorts of treasures can be found. Their catalogue lists such temptations as bush green beans, Fin de Bagnols, Triomphe de Farcy, Roi des Belges, bush yellow beans and Beurre de Bocquencourt, nice to plant side by side and pretty to serve together when they are so tiny that the beans can be eaten whole; green flageolets Chevrier, used in the following recipe; celeraric, or root celery, a small *mâche*, Green Full Heart, most delicate of salad greens; leeks, lovely lettuces, salsify and shallots, Petits Pois Provençals, melons and courgettes, all very tempting to the amateur gardener and cook. If you garden you will enjoy their catalogue. If you don't they carry as well a large group of delicacies for the table, from foie gras to *fleurs cristallisées*.

FLAGEOLETS FINES HERBES

SERVES 8–10

1 pound dried flageolets
5 cups water
1 onion, chopped
3 cloves garlic, mashed
4 or 5 cloves
2 teaspoons salt
4 tablespoons butter
Tabasco
freshly ground black pepper
fresh minced herbs (parsley, chervil, sweet marjoram, basil, thyme,
  as available)

Rinse the beans and soak for several hours or overnight in the water. Drain; cover with fresh water. Add the onion, garlic, cloves and salt and simmer over low heat until the beans are tender, about 2 hours. Season to taste with the butter, Tabasco, freshly ground black pepper and minced herbs. Serve with roast lamb and its pan gravy.

AUBERGINES TOULOUSIENNES

SERVES 8

2 good-sized eggplants
salt
flour
olive oil
2 cloves garlic, crushed
4 sprigs parsley, chopped
3 tomatoes, thinly sliced
1 cup small cubes bread

Peel and slice the eggplants, salt each slice lightly, and let stand for an hour or two. Pour off any accumulated liquid. Dip each slice in flour and fry in hot oil until golden. Remove to a hot platter. Put the garlic and parsley in the oil and in the oil fry the tomatoes. Arrange them over the eggplant. Add more oil and sauté the bread cubes until crisp. Drain them on absorbent paper, pour over the eggplant and serve.

DATE PUDDING

A fine party dessert, this is best prepared in the morning or the day before and served at room temperature, covered with cold whipped cream. It is chewy and rich and the recipe never fails.

1 cup sugar
2½ tablespoons flour
2 egg whites, beaten stiff
1 teaspoon baking powder
1 cup coarsely chopped nuts
1 cup chopped dates
2 tablespoons sour cream
2 egg yolks, beaten
1 pint sweetened whipped cream, flavored to taste with vanilla extract

Preheat oven to 400° F.

Mix the ingredients, adding the egg yolks last, and bake in a large (preferably 10 inch) Pyrex pie pan set in another pan of water for 40 minutes. When you take the pudding out of the oven it will fall. Cool it and cut it into wedges. Before serving heap it with sweetened, vanilla-flavored whipped cream.

MENU VII

Cream of Sorrel Soup

Beef Tongue with Mustard Cream
Herbed Mashed Potatoes
Braised Endive
Carrots Vichy

Délice d'Abricots with Chocolate Curls

A fine red Bordeaux will complement the beef tongue.

CREAM OF SORREL SOUP

SERVES 8

1 stick sweet butter
1 onion, peeled and chopped
2 teaspoons cornstarch
5 cups chicken stock
1 pound fresh sorrel, washed and dried, tough stems removed
2 sprigs parsley, chopped
2 egg yolks
salt and pepper
2 cups light cream

Melt the butter in a large pot, add the onion and sauté until translucent, about 5 minutes, then stir in the cornstarch and cook for 5 minutes longer. Gradually add the chicken stock and then, a handful at a time, the sorrel and the parsley. Simmer gently for about 20 minutes, uncovered. Remove from the heat and stir in the egg yolks, salt and pepper. Cool the soup and purée it in a food processor or a blender, then strain it through a chinois or a fine sieve. The soup may be served chilled or hot. If cold, add the cream just before serving. If hot, reheat the soup with the cream.

BEEF TONGUE WITH MUSTARD CREAM

SERVES 8

1 (4–5-pound) smoked beef tongue
water to cover
½ lemon, sliced
1 onion, studded with cloves
1 stalk celery, cut up
1 carrot, sliced
1 bay leaf

Rinse the beef tongue, cover it with water and add the other ingredients.
Simmer, covered, until tender, about 3 hours. Cool the tongue, remove the
root and skin it. Serve on a warm platter, garnished, and pass hot Mustard
Cream.

MUSTARD CREAM

1 PINT

1 (8-ounce) jar Dijon mustard, Moutarde en graine or green pepper
  mustard
8 ounces Crème Fraîche (see Index)

Mix together and serve hot. The texture and flavor can be varied to suit
your whim according to the mustard used.

CARROTS VICHY

2½ pounds carrots
¾ teaspoon salt
2 tablespoons sugar
finely chopped parsley
5 tablespoons butter
½ cup chicken broth
parsley for garnish

Preheat oven to 375°F.

Scrape carrots and slice them as thin as possible. Spread a third of them in a shallow, buttered cocotte, sprinkle with a third of the salt and a third of the sugar and the chopped parsley and dot with a third of the butter. Repeat for 2 more layers. Pour the broth over all, cover cocotte closely and bring to a boil. Place in oven and cook for about 35 minutes. Garnish with parsley.

DÉLICE D'ABRICOTS

SERVES 8–10

1 pound dried apricots
water to cover
sugar to taste
2 tablespoons apricot brandy
½ pint heavy cream
4 egg whites
Chocolate Curls for garnish

Soak the apricots in the water and cook them until soft. Add sugar and apricot brandy and purée the mixture in a food processor or blender until smooth and light. Whip the cream until it forms fairly stiff peaks and fold half of it into the apricot purée. Chill. Just before serving beat the egg whites until stiff and fold them into the purée. Last, fold in the remaining whipped cream, barely mixing, so that a pretty marbelized effect results. Pile lightly in a cold serving dish and garnish with Chocolate Curls.

CHOCOLATE CURLS

Place a square of bitter chocolate in a warm place (a gas oven with pilot light burning is very satisfactory) until the chocolate has been slightly softened. Shave it with a vegetable peeler; longer strokes make longer curls. Use to decorate cakes or other desserts.

MENU VIII

FOR 8

---

with cocktails:
Crudités, Salted Nuts, Mushroom Sandwiches

Billi-Bi
Cheese Straws (see Index)

Tournedos Dauphinois
Braised Celery
Brussels Sprouts with Brazil Nuts
Potatoes Rissolées

Ginger Roll

A fine red Burgundy with the Tournedos

BILLI-BI

SERVES 8

A beautiful, beautiful soup which was invented by Martin Decré of La Côte Basque and La Caravelle, traditionally two of our finest restaurants!

4 pounds fresh, scrubbed mussels
1 onion, chopped
3 shallots, chopped
3 sprigs parsley
2 tablespoons butter
1 pint dry white wine
salt, pepper and dash cayenne
1 quart heavy cream

Cook together for 10 minutes all the ingredients except the cream. Remove the mussel shells and strain through cheesecloth. (Reserve the mussels for another delicious bite.)

Return to the stove before serving and stir in the heavy cream. Simmer, without boiling, and serve very hot with Cheese Straws (*see Index*).

TOURNEDOS DAUPHINOIS

SERVES 8

1 pound firm white mushrooms, trimmed and cleaned
1½ sticks butter
salt
freshly ground white pepper
1 tablespoon flour
1 cup warm cream
8 tournedos (slices of beef tenderloin cut 1 inch thick)
8 slices French bread
½ cup port wine

Slice the mushrooms and sauté them in ½ stick of the butter until the liquid is evaporated. Sprinkle them with salt, pepper and flour and blend well. Stir in the cream and blend until smooth. Keep hot.

Meanwhile quickly sauté the tournedos in another ½ stick butter, turning until they are brown but still rare inside. Sauté the slices of bread in the remaining ½ stick butter, turning until they are evenly toasted. Put the tournedos on the bread and arrange them in a ring on a heated platter. Pour the mushrooms in the center. Make a sauce by stirring port into the juices in the pan; season to taste with salt and pepper, pour a spoonful on each tournedo and serve.

POTATOES RISSOLÉES

SERVES 8

8 large potatoes
½ cup butter
salt

Perhaps 10 medium-sized potatoes may be required for this recipe as the potatoes are shaped by cutting them with a medium-sized melon-ball cutter.

After shaping the potatoes, parboil them for 4–5 minutes. Drain them and place them in a sauté pan in which the butter has been melted. Cook, shaking and rolling them in the butter until brown all over. Salt to taste.

GINGER ROLL

SERVES 8

1 cup flour
1 teaspoon ground ginger
1 teaspoon ground cinnamon
1 teaspoon ground nutmeg
1 teaspoon ground allspice
1 teaspoon baking soda
⅓ cup melted butter
⅓ cup molasses
⅓ cup sugar or light corn syrup
1 egg, well beaten
½ cup hot water
a little confectioners' sugar
1 pint heavy cream, whipped

Preheat oven to 350° F.

Mix the flour, spices and baking soda in a bowl. Add the melted butter, molasses, sugar or corn syrup, egg and hot water. Mix well.

Butter a cookie sheet, line with waxed paper and butter again. Spread the batter lightly over the buttered waxed paper. Bake for 15 minutes, or until just set. Remove and cover with a cloth that has been wrung out in cold water. Cool in the refrigerator. Remove the cloth and dust well with confectioners' sugar. Turn out on waxed paper and carefully peel the paper off the top. Spread with whipped cream and roll up like a jelly roll. Serve on a long, narrow wooden board.

JUST A BITE

Short-order cooking with a silver spoon, these menus take care of those spontaneous occasions when there just isn't much time for either cooking or eating—a light supper or luncheon, something to go with a pre-theater bracer, a midnight supper or times when you just feel like staying away from the kitchen. All of these are good things to eat. The menus work well amidst the exciting conflict of backgammon, bridge or Chicago, when someone comes in unexpectedly, or when the family is together at home.

If you set up a buffet with the needed accessories ahead of time, these meals should prove carefree and sustaining.

In this chapter, I have given quite a lot of choice because, in most of our lives, these occasions occur pretty frequently. Because of the informality of planning, you can switch things about easily or augment a menu if there's time for a little more leisurely eating.

Desserts should not be a problem. Interesting fruits, ices and ice creams, cookies and pastries are available just a step away, and some of the fine baked goods on your grocer's shelves are of high quality, too. So all of the dessert suggestions in the chapter are presumed to be bought or assembled ahead of time. I have put desserts in parentheses because they may be used or not as time allows. Anyway, they're easy.

Recently I received a constantly useful present from Lisa, my daughter—beautifully real-looking pottery pears (they come from Bendel's). They have removable tops and can be filled with something nice, and chilled or frozen until needed. The effect, when they are produced on a large Creuil platter, is so pretty that anything they hold tastes, somehow, better. Most often it is an ice cream or sherbet spiked with a fruit syrup or liqueur. Fresh berries or nuts can be added just before serving and ripe mangoes to top vanilla or peach ice cream. The pale green of avocado soup or pink shrimp soup is effective too. Little covered dishes of many sorts are to be found and you'll have another course on hand with no trouble at all.

The other day I dropped in, unannounced, on Donald Bruce White. While still young, he became the acknowledged dean of New York's frenetic catering scene. From his opulent house in the Sixties, he keeps an unforgiving eye on his large, well-trained staff. There, like a pasha, he lunched me beautifully. This was it. One dry martini, a few mouthfuls of pearl-gray caviar on hot buttered toast and an omelette that was light, pale and tender, enclosing a cream-dressed filling of fresh spinach. Rich, perfect coffee, small cookies, easy conversation, that's all. But this is a small example of what I am trying to say in this book. Just that simple, just that great—people who enjoy each other, together, laughing, eating good food.

When Donald was just beginning, by the way, he used to come over to our house and stick an expensive roast in the oven when his own shaky oven had gone on the fritz. In return, he'd send a meat pie of rare savor or a blooming camellia tree. "Return" is a meaningful word in friendship.

Herewith a baker's dozen of recipes to try when time is short. The food can easily be managed, rich or light; it is okay if it is what you'd like to eat yourself, quiet hospitality, quiet service, quiet food.

MENU I

FOR 4 OR 5

Veal and Chicken Pejarsky
Hazelnut Butter
Dinner Rolls
Carrot and Yogurt Salad

(Forgotten Torte)

VEAL AND CHICKEN PEJARSKY

SERVES 4–5

A recipe of Chef Martin Decré, when he was at La Côte Basque, New York City. (Now M. Decré has moved to La Caravelle.)

½ pound boneless veal
½ pound boneless chicken breast
½ pint heavy cream
1¼ cups very fine fresh bread crumbs, slightly moistened with some of
the heavy cream
clarified butter

Fill a mixing bowl with cracked ice and let stand until thoroughly chilled. Grind the chicken and veal together very fine and put in bowl which has been emptied and wiped dry. Add the moistened bread crumbs. With a wooden spatula mix thoroughly, adding the heavy cream slowly and mixing vigorously until the mixture forms into a stiff compact mass. With a large spoon form balls according to the size desired and roll these in fresh bread crumbs. Then flatten them hamburger style and fry in a pan over a low flame in clarified butter. Serve with hazelnut butter.

HAZELNUT BUTTER

6 OUNCES

2 ounces hazelnuts
4 ounces butter

Grind the nuts fine in the food processor, add the butter and blend well. Remove and chill until needed.

CARROT AND YOGURT SALAD

May also be used as an addition to a buffet or hors d'oeuvre tray.

1 pound carrots, scraped and cleaned
mayonnaise
yogurt
salt
parsley, watercress or finely diced peaches for garnish

Put the carrots through the fine grater of the food processor or grate them by hand, medium fine. Add the other ingredients to taste. Chill, garnish and serve.

FORGOTTEN TORTE

SERVES 5–6

5 egg whites
¼ teaspoon of salt
½ teaspoon cream of tartar
1½ cups sugar
1 teaspoon vanilla extract
1 pint vanilla ice cream
1 pint strawberries, hulled, cleaned, sliced and sweetened

Preheat oven to 450° F.

Beat egg whites until frothy, sprinkle salt and cream of tartar over top and beat until stiff. Gradually beat in sugar 2 tablespoons at a time. Add vanilla extract and continue to beat until mixture forms peaks. Pour into a well-buttered springform pan. Place torte in oven. Then turn off heat at once! Bake overnight in stored-up heat. Do not remove torte until the following morning. Serve with ice cream and fresh strawberries over the top. The torte is even better the second day.

MENU II

Calf's Liver Sautéed in Pistachio Nuts
Potatoes Rissolées (see Index)
Watercress Salad
Melba Toast

Compote of Figs with Heavy Cream

CALF'S LIVER SAUTÉED IN PISTACHIO NUTS

SERVES 4

1½ pounds calf's liver, sliced thin
1 cup pistachio nuts, finely chopped
salt to taste
fresh ground black pepper to taste
6 tablespoons butter
grated orange peel for garnish
bacon for garnish (optional)
tomatoes for garnish

Carefully dip the slices of calf's liver in ground nuts on a cutting board so that the slices are evenly coated all over. Season with salt and pepper. Sauté the slices, 2 at a time, in a tablespoon or two of butter. In order to produce a nice brown crust avoid using too much butter at one time. Arrange the calf's liver slices on a hot platter, grate orange peel over them and garnish with crisp bacon if you wish, green parsley or watercress, small red broiled tomatoes or black olives—whatever looks pretty and is at hand. Serve hot with Potatoes Rissolées.

COMPOTE OF FIGS

An easy dessert, a pleasant combination of tastes and textures.

fresh or glass jars of figs (12 figs)
kirsch
Crème Fraîche (see Index)
candied ginger
almonds

Wash and dry the fresh figs or drain the glassed ones. Arrange in a compote or serving bowl and pour over them a little kirsch. Mask the fruit with Crème Fraîche and chill the dish until serving time. Sliver ginger over the dish and add whole blanched almonds. Sprinkle on top the coarse sugar that comes with the ginger.

Park Avenue Pot Roast
(Coupe Chicago)

PARK AVENUE POT ROAST

SERVES 6

1 (5-pound) pot roast
flour
salt and black pepper to taste
2 tablespoons butter
2 tablespoons peanut oil
1 pound onions, chopped
3 cloves garlic, mashed
water
red wine
1 pound baby carrots, washed and scraped
1 pound turnips, washed, scraped and cut into pieces
Kitchen Bouquet (optional)
1 pound narrow noodles
½ pound small white mushrooms
chopped parsley

Dredge the pot roast in flour seasoned with salt and black pepper and brown it in a heavy pot or Dutch oven in the butter and oil. Reduce the heat, add the onions and cook to brown lightly. Add the garlic and enough water and red wine to cover the roast. Cover the pot tightly and simmer the roast over very low heat for 3–4 hours, stirring occasionally and turning the meat.

Add the carrots and turnips to the pot and again simmer gently for ½ hour, stirring occasionally. The gravy will now be thick and smooth. If necessary, add more wine and, if you like, Kitchen Bouquet to color.

Add noodles and mushrooms to the pot roast and simmer for 10 minutes longer, until the noodles are tender. Arrange roast on a large hot platter. Correct seasoning. Surround roast with the vegetables and garnish with parsley.

COUPE CHICAGO

SERVES 6

This is the best of all the combinations I have hit upon to present in those little pottery pears mentioned earlier. Everyone loves chocolate anyway, and here it is in subtle company. Set the desserts in the freezer and whip them out at the last minute. I first made the concoction for an evening when we were playing Chicago, that variation on bridge which requires a very high degree of concentration, so I named the recipe for that wonderful game. It is rich, so the servings are small ones.

1½ pints finest chocolate ice cream
1 (6-ounce) jar Raffetto Brandied Marron Pieces
kirsch to taste
6 tablespoons ginger marmalade
6 tablespoons chocolate sauce (see Index)

Divide the ice cream among 6 cups that can go in the freezer. Add to each a tablespoonful of the marron pieces and a dash of kirsch. Mix together the ginger marmalade and the chocolate sauce, and just before serving, pour it, hot, over the iced desserts. A rapturous little afterthought.

MENU IV

Chicken Hash à la Ritz
Wild Rice
French Bread
Bibb Lettuce and Walnut Salad

(Stilton Apple Tart)

CHICKEN HASH À LA RITZ

SERVES 4–5

Didi Lorillard gave me this recipe of her grandmother's. Like Didi, Mrs. Lorillard was a great hostess and cook. She cooked the old-fashioned way by carefully supervising the work of a professional in the kitchen. This recipe comes from the Ritz in Paris. It is very delicate.

2 pairs chicken breasts
water to cover
1 small onion, sliced
1 small stalk celery
½ teaspoon salt
5 peppercorns
1 bay leaf
1 teaspoon dried tarragon leaves

Simmer the chicken breasts in water with the above ingredients until done, about 20 minutes. Skin, bone and cut the meat in bite-size pieces. Put meat in a saucepan with:

1 cup heavy cream

Cook until the cream is reduced by half. Set aside.

2 tablespoons butter
2 tablespoons flour
1 cup milk
salt and white pepper to taste
1½ tablespoons heavy cream
¼ teaspoon tarragon leaves
¼ cup dry white wine

Over low heat cook together the butter and flour until the flour is pale gold. Slowly, while stirring, add the milk.

Cook, stirring with a wire whisk, until the sauce is very thick. Stir in the cream, tarragon and the wine.

Add ½ cup of this sauce to the chicken and arrange in a buttered shallow baking dish. To the remaining sauce add:

1 beaten egg yolk
2 tablespoons whipped cream

Combine egg yolk and whipped cream; pour mixture over the hash and brown quickly under the broiler and serve.

STILTON APPLE TART

A nice variation on the ever popular and useful quiche.

Pastry for a 9-inch pie crust
4 eggs, lightly beaten
2 cups light cream or half and half
¼ teaspoon grated nutmeg
½ teaspoon salt
¼ teaspoon white pepper
1 cup crumbled Stilton cheese
1 tablespoon port wine
1 tart apple

Preheat oven to 450° F.

Line a pie plate with the crust and bake for 5 minutes. Combine the eggs, cream, nutmeg, salt and pepper, add the cheese and port wine and pour into the pie. Pare and core the apple and slice it neatly over the pie. Bake for 15 minutes, reduce the heat to 350° and continue baking until a knife inserted in the pie comes out clean, about 10 minutes. Serve hot.

MENU V

FOR 4

(*Cucumber-Yogurt Soup*)

Steak Tartare
Salade Variée
Watercress Dressing
Hot Buttered Pumpernickel

(*Honeydew Melon with Cantelope Ice*)
(*Date Bars* [see Index])

Serve cold beer with the tartare and hot espresso with the dessert.

STEAK TARTARE

SERVES 4

This is one of my favorites but you have to know your audience, for there are some who simply will not eat steak tartare. What they are missing! For those who can't eat it raw, I sometimes provide a small hotplate on the side and let them cook it themselves. We have little jokes about cannibals and missionaries. Cannibals may have icy beer but missionaries are supposed to drink hot tea.

This allows ½ pound steak per person. It should be ground, either at home or by a good butcher, just (within an hour) before serving.

2 pounds freshly ground sirloin tip or top round, without fat
2 teaspoons salt
black pepper to taste
1 cup finely minced Bermuda onions
4 egg yolks
capers for garnish
4 rolled anchovy fillets
2 lemons
parsley for garnish

Toss together lightly the meat, salt, pepper and ½ cup of the minced onions. Arrange portions on chilled plates. Make an indentation in each portion and slip an egg yolk into it. Sprinkle capers over the meat and garnish with a rolled anchovy fillet. Put a lemon half, more chopped Bermuda onions and parsley around it and serve with a pepper grinder and Worcestershire or Tabasco sauce for those who like them, although these strong condiments seem to defeat the point of the dish, which is the fresh sweet taste of the meat.

SALADE VARIÉE

summer lettuces, buttercrunch, Bibb or oak-leaf
whole basil leaves
Watercress Dressing (recipe follows)
1 large avocado
tomatoes, sliced in generous pieces
black olives
pistachio nuts, chopped

Wash and dry the lettuce and basil, leaving the basil leaves whole as they do in Italy. Toss in Watercress Dressing and arrange in a large glass or lucite bowl. Peel and cube the avocado; marinate in Watercress Dressing. Arrange the avocado, tomatoes and black olives over the lettuce. Garnish with the chopped pistachio nuts.

WATERCRESS DRESSING

½ cup olive oil
1 tablespoon cider vinegar
½ bunch watercress, washed, coarse stems removed and dried
½ clove garlic
salt to taste
a handful of blanched almonds

This dressing must be made in an electric blender or food processor. Whirl all ingredients except almonds until thoroughly mixed and light. The specks of watercress will coat the salad and lend their flavor to it. Sliver a handful of blanched almonds into the salad. This makes enough dressing for 2 heads of Boston lettuce. Also good on endive.

MENU VI

Lobster and Fish Chowder
Hot Garlic Bread

Salade aux Haricots Verts

(Walnut Cake)

LOBSTER AND FISH CHOWDER

SERVES 4 OR 5

This chowder, served with some good bread, toasted buttered crackers or pita bread, makes a marvelous main dish for supper or a light meal.

1 lobster, 1½–1¾ pounds
salted water
1 stalk celery, sliced
1 bay leaf
1 large onion, diced
1 tablespoon butter
3 potatoes, peeled and finely diced
¾ pound boneless fillet of fluke or flounder
1 pint light cream
freshly ground white pepper, to taste
chopped herbs, dill, chives and chervil, as available
1 jigger sherry or ½ jigger anisette (optional)

Steam the lobster in a small amount of salted water with the celery and bay leaf until cooked a bright red, 10–12 minutes. Remove the lobster, cool it and remove the meat from the shell. Cut it in cubes and reserve. Return the lobster shell to the stock, adding a little more water and cook for ½ hour. Strain the lobster stock and discard the shell.

Cook the onion in the butter gently until translucent. Add the potatoes. Cook until the potatoes are soft. Cube the fish and add to the stock. Cook for a few minutes. Add the diced lobster meat and the cream and stir together over low heat until blended. Season to taste; add white pepper. Serve hot, garnished with finely minced herbs. If you like, sherry or anisette can be added at the last.

SALADE AUX HARICOTS VERTS

SERVES 4

From New York's famous restaurant, La Grenouille.

1½ pounds fresh haricots verts or young, tender green beans
2–3 quarts boiling water
⅓ cup vegetable oil
2 tablespoons raspberry vinegar
3 shallots, finely minced
salt, freshly ground pepper, to taste
1 teaspoon finely chopped chervil or 1–2 tablespoons chopped parsley

Trim haricots verts and cook about 5 minutes in rapidly boiling water. They must retain their crispness. Drain and cool slightly. Blend oil and vinegar and pour over the green beans. Add the chopped shallots and season with a little salt and lots of freshly ground pepper. Top with chervil or parsley.

NOTE It is important to serve the salad at room temperature because chilling will lessen the delicate flavors.

WALNUT CAKE

In a ring mold bake a yellow Duncan Hines cake according to the package instructions, adding ½ cup ground walnuts and ½ teaspoon vanilla. After baking, unmold and decorate the cake with whole walnut halves. Glaze the cake with melted apricot jam to which you can, if you like, add rum. Serve warm or chilled with cold whipped cream.

MENU VII

This menu was planned for a pre-theater party by Mrs. E. Williams Holmes. Eve, who is my close friend, has moved from her house in the country to a small, stylish apartment in town. Here on Park Avenue, she entertains with the same flair she has always had. It is a quick but elegant little dinner.

Filet de Boeuf
Béarnaise Sauce (see Index)
Confiture de Tomates
Small Baked Potatoes
Warm Spinach Salad

(*Chocolate and Praline Mousse*)

CONFITURE DE TOMATES

2 (8-OUNCE) JARS

Adapted from a recipe which Eve found in Haiti.

2 pounds tomatoes
1 cup water
2 pounds sugar
1 vanilla bean
lemon rind
¼ cup slivered almonds

Boil sugar in water until dissolved. Peel tomatoes and cut into quarters; place in sugar water along with vanilla bean and lemon rind. Cook for 30–45 minutes, then add almonds. Pour in 2 jars. Chill to set.

CHOCOLATE AND PRALINE MOUSSE

SERVES 6

La Folie (in the Hotel Carlton, heir to the old Ritz) is one of New York's handsomest restaurants and the food there is wonderful. A wide and interesting choice of dishes is always beautifully prepared and presented in a luxurious and glamorous setting: pilasters of real malachite stand against a background of mirrors. The floors are marble, the lighting varies from subtle at lunchtime to psychedelic after dinner. This is their imaginative variation on everyone's all-time favorite, a feathery chocolate mousse.

3 ounces unsweetened chocolate
2 ounces semisweet chocolate
⅓ cup praline, coarsely ground
4 egg yolks
4 egg whites
pinch cream of tartar
¾ cups sugar
½ cup heavy cream, whipped until it holds stiff peaks

In the top of a double boiler set over hot water, melt the chocolates and cool to lukewarm. Add the praline powder and the egg yolks, one at a time, beating after each addition. In a large bowl beat the egg whites with the cream of tartar until they hold soft peaks. Beat in the sugar, 2 tablespoons at a time, beating the meringue until it holds stiff peaks. Beat half the meringue into the chocolate mixture; fold in the remaining meringue and the whipped cream. Pour the mousse into a serving bowl and chill for several hours or overnight.

MENU VIII

FOR 4 OR 5

(Cold Crème Senegalese)
Chafing-Dish Scrambled Eggs with Smoked Salmon on
Buttered Toast Points
Watercress and Endive Salad
Blue Cheese Dressing
(Fresh Unhulled Strawberries, Crème Fraîche [see Index]*)*

COLD CRÈME SENEGALESE

SERVES 4–5

The concoction of Sarah Y. Reuschler of the Chelsea penthouse gallery of that name.

Don't be offended by the idea of canned soups in this hot-weather thriller. The texture and flavor always receive raves. The recipe allows a little for seconds, usually needed.

1 can cream of chicken soup
1 can cream of celery soup
1 can chicken consommé
3 tablespoons onion juice
½ cup lemon juice
curry paste to your taste, but a lot of it
ginger likewise
½ cup white wine
1 cup heavy cream
garnish:
   freshly sautéed garlic croutons
   chopped toasted almonds
   chopped green peppers
   grated orange rind
   chopped chives

The soup will have to be made in 2 or 3 batches in a blender or food processor. The division may be approximate, as they will all be combined in the end. Combine the first 7 ingredients and mix in batches until light. Pour together in a large bowl. Stir in the wine and cream and chill for a long time in the refrigerator—6 hours or overnight.

Serve the soup in a punch bowl which has been chilled with ice or, if you wish, serve over a block of ice. Surround the bowl with little dishes containing the garnishes listed above and serve. (Mortimer's, the popular and chic café on Lexington Avenue at 75th Street serves their creamy Senegalese garnished with a slice of apple and freshly grated coconut.)

CHAFING-DISH SCRAMBLED EGGS

Although a lot of attention has been focused in recent years on the perfect omelette, somehow scrambled eggs, first cousin and just as delicate, just as versatile and just as good, perhaps better, seem to have been forgotten. There is one restaurant in Paris, Jamin, which has built a reputation on this simple, perfect dish. You can do just as well at home as Jamin does in its elegant surroundings just off the rue François Ière in the 16th arrondissement. Fresh eggs, fresh butter and hot porcelain plates are necessary.

For each portion, and up to 6 can be cooked together in a chafing dish, mix 2 lightly beaten eggs with 1 tablespoon water. For each portion allow ½ tablespoon sweet butter to melt slowly and coat the pan. Pour in the eggs, diluted with water and cook as slowly as possible, stirring slightly until just set. Add a dash of coarse salt and serve on hot plates.

Scrambled eggs are wonderful poured over a slice of hot toast or accompanied by toast points that have just been buttered. Parsley, watercress, chives, almost any fresh green, finely minced, makes an appropriate garnish.

This simple procedure can be varied by the addition of 1 tablespoon creamy cottage cheese to each portion, garnished with grated orange rind or finely cut herbs. For more important presentations, try them with smoked salmon. Prince Charles sometimes scrambles his this way. Other ingredients might be crab meat, a little ham of good quality, creamed chicken, asparagus tips, etc. A dash of sour cream and caviar can be heavenly. Just remember to scramble the eggs as slowly and lightly as possible and to serve them immediately, very hot.

MENU IX

FOR 4

(Avocado Soup)

Fettucini with Pesto
Greens Salad

(Persimmons)
(Caramel Nuggets [see Index]*)*

AVOCADO SOUP

SERVES 4

A lovely cool green soup, full of health.

1 large ripe avocado
1 small boiled potato
1 teaspoon minced onion
1 tablespoon lemon juice
1 cup yogurt
½ teaspoon salt
several dashes Tabasco
1½ cups chicken broth
chopped toasted almonds for garnish
snipped dill or chervil for garnish

Combine the first 7 ingredients in food processor or blender and purée together until smooth. Combine with the chicken broth. Chill thoroughly,
garnish with chopped toasted almonds and snipped dill or chervil and serve.

FETTUCINI WITH PESTO

Wonderful fresh pasta in a delightfully wide array of sizes and shapes and colors is available thanks to Pasta & Cheese, Zabar's and a number of other shops dotted around town. This phenomenon is a great boon to the host or hostess in a hurry. Nothing could be simpler than to pick up pasta, a "home-made" sauce and bread, there, at the eleventh hour. One pound of pasta serves five people well.

1 *pound fettucini, green, white or orange-colored, or a mixture of all three*
rapidly boiling salted water
Pesto (recipe follows)
Parmesan cheese, grated

Cook the fettucini for just 3 minutes in rapidly boiling salted water, drain and toss with Pesto to your taste. Serve immediately on very hot plates and pass freshly grated Parmesan cheese.

PESTO

ABOUT 1¾ CUPS

Pesto can be bought freshly prepared in the shops mentioned in the preceding recipe. However, during the summer when I have masses of basil in the garden, or at times when it is available in quantity in the market, I make it from scratch and freeze it.

In a blender or food processor with steel blade, purée:

3 cups coarsely chopped basil leaves
1 cup pine nuts
flat-leaved parsley to taste
¾ cup grated Parmesan cheese
½ cup olive oil
1 clove garlic
salt and pepper to taste

MENU X

Chicken Breasts Cordon Bleu
Broiled Mushrooms
Basil and Tomato Salad

(Vanilla Ice Cream with Mangoes)
(Cookies)

CHICKEN BREASTS CORDON BLEU

SERVES 6

This method of preparing a famous Cordon Bleu dish was perfected by a skillful amateur chef, George Mittendorf. It works like a breeze as a very stylish little bite.

3 chicken breasts, halved and boned
flour
salt and pepper to taste
2 eggs, lightly beaten
seasoned bread crumbs
6 thin slices ham
1 cup grated Swiss cheese
heavy cream

Have your butcher halve and bone the chicken breasts, or do it yourself, it is not hard. Place the breasts, skinned side down on a wooden board, cover with Saran wrap and flatten with a wooden mallet. Dip the chicken in flour to coat, then in beaten egg and finally in seasoned bread crumbs. Fill the interior of each with a thin slice of ham, grated Swiss cheese and moisten the interior with a little heavy cream. Fold the pieces of chicken, corners to center, envelope fashion, 4 times and secure by pressing firmly. You should have neat little square packages. These may now be Saran-wrapped and stored until needed in the refrigerator, or frozen for a later occasion.

To serve, bring the portions to room temperature, then sauté in a good quantity of butter until golden brown on both sides and cooked through.

Vealburgers in Mustard Cream
Broiled Tomatoes
Toasted French Rolls

(Casaba Melon with Raspberries)
(Pecan Crisps [see Index])

VEALBURGERS IN MUSTARD CREAM

SERVES 4 OR 5

Really heaven-sent, these are as quick and easy as anything you can prepare but delicate and still unusual—a fine dish with only a moment's thought and one with nice contrasts. As the veal is tender, the interior should be rare and juicy, the exterior crusty brown. The meat needs no seasoning but a little onion juice. The sauce is smooth and very sharp.

2 tablespoons onion juice
2 pounds ground veal, of good quality with little fat
6 tablespoons sweet butter
½ cup Dijon mustard
½ cup heavy cream
1 tablespoon lemon juice
butter
6 rolled anchovies
watercress or parsley for garnish

Mix the onion juice with the veal and shape into 6 cylindrical patties, about 1½ inches thick, flat on top and bottom and straight on the sides. Sauté in the butter over brisk heat, turning until you have a nice crust on each side of the patties and have reached the desired stage of doneness. A juicy interior is desirable. Remove the meat to a warm plate while you make the sauce by stirring the mustard, cream and lemon juice into the pan juices and blend them well together. Pour the sauce onto a hot platter and arrange the patties on it. Dot with butter and top each with an anchovy. Garnish with watercress or parsley and serve.

MENU XII

Linguine with Fresh Clam Sauce
Italian Bread
Caesar Salad

(Strawberry Pie)

LINGUINE WITH CLAM SAUCE

SERVES 4 OR 5

Delicious with fresh clams, this recipe is one of those that is easy to multiply or divide as you wish.

18 cherrystone clams
1 stick sweet butter
4 tablespoons finely chopped parsley
4 tablespoons finely chopped basil
1 cup heavy cream
2 cloves garlic, mashed
freshly ground pepper

Rinse the clams well; open them, saving all the juice, and chop them. If you wish, a brief whirl in a food processor will accomplish this trick. Put the clams with the butter into a saucepan and stir over a low flame. Gradually add the other ingredients and stir to reduce slightly.

1 pound fresh linguine
sliced white truffles
freshly grated Parmesan or Romano cheese

In rapidly boiling salted water cook the linguine, *al dente*, 2 or 3 minutes. Drain. The pasta may now be divided into 4 or 5 individual portions and served on hot plates with the sauce, truffles and Parmesan, or all of these may be mixed together in a buttered chafing dish and served with an added flourish.

CAESAR SALAD

This ever popular salad has a unique and appealing combination of ingredients. I like the addition of rolled anchovies as a garnish, but this is only a personal taste.

1 clove garlic
1 teaspoon salt
freshly ground pepper
⅓ cup olive oil
juice of 1½ lemons
1 tablespoon red wine vinegar
1 raw egg
Worcestershire sauce to taste
3 medium heads romaine lettuce, washed, dried, crisped and torn into
    bite-size pieces
1 cup freshly made croutons, sautéed in olive oil
freshly grated Parmesan cheese
rolled anchovies (optional)

Rub a salad bowl with the clove of garlic. Add the salt, pepper, olive oil, lemon juice, vinegar, egg and Worcestershire sauce. Beat with a whisk until creamy. Add the lettuce and croutons and toss. Add the cheese and toss again. Serve immediately, garnished, if you like, with anchovies.

STRAWBERRY PIE

For a carefree splurge, try this delectation from Eles Gillet!

1 cup sugar
3½ tablespoons cornstarch
pinch salt
1 cup crushed strawberries
½ stick butter
¼ cup water
1 baked 9-inch pie shell (see Index)
1 (3-ounce) package cream cheese, softened
1 cup whole perfect strawberries
1 cup whipped cream
¼ teaspoon almond extract
2 tablespoons confectioners' sugar

Combine first 6 ingredients in a saucepan; cook until thick and transparent, stirring constantly. Cool. Spread pie shell with softened cream cheese. Stand whole strawberries in cream cheese to completely cover the bottom of the pie shell. Spread cooled sauce over strawberries. Cover with whipped cream to which almond extract and confectioners' sugar have been added. Chill.

MENU XIII

FOR 4

This one is planned for a *really* quick bite where you have just time for a cocktail or two before dashing out.

Macadamia Nuts
Celery and Olives

Park Avenue Hamburgers

PARK AVENUE HAMBURGERS

SERVES 4

These miniature hamburgers were first made for Ted Peckham, who considers them the best pre-theater snack, bar none, that one can have. He named them and eats them regularly. They are marvelously good and easy for a bit of nourishment before the theater—or afterward, if you must wait that long.

1½ pounds ground sirloin steak
1 egg yolk
2 tablespoons minced Bermuda onion
1 scant teaspoon salt
juice of ½ lemon
3 tablespoons sweet butter
12 poppyseed rolls, toasted and spread with sweet butter
2 ounces caviar
12 oysters
green Madagascar peppercorns
watercress and tomatoes for garnish

Mix the ground steak thoroughly with the egg yolk, minced onion, salt and lemon juice and form into 12 small thick patties. Cook quickly in sweet butter until the exteriors are brown, the centers still rare. Meanwhile, toast and butter the poppyseed rolls and place on a hot platter. Make a small indentation in each hamburger and fill it with a small spoonful of caviar. Place an oyster on top, sprinkle with a few green Madagascar peppercorns and set the hamburgers on the bottom halves of the rolls. Leave the tops of the rolls at the side; the dish will look prettier that way. Serve hot, surrounded with watercress and tomato slices.

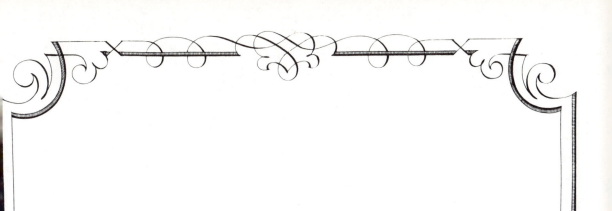

BIG
PARTIES

Into each successful life there comes a day when everyone is coming to *your* house—before the theater or after a game, to celebrate a wedding or a reunion to fête visiting friends. This is your time to shine.

In New York as in most cities, it is possible to get a caterer to fend but, really, there is nothing more hospitable and heartwarming than a meal that is cooked at home. It's just different. The house smells just a bit of good food and the aura of hospitality wafts through the air, with the soft music (or loud music, if that is your bag). Speaking of that, a little live music can usually be obtained and adds more than its share to the festivities.

To make life easy and so that you can have time to enjoy yourself, you should have a simple and foolproof menu. At certain times, those dear old friends, the big Tom turkey or a well-presented ham, or both, are needed. At other times, big cassoulets or tureens of chili are quite enough. But here are somewhat more unusual ideas. All these menus can be gotten ready in advance so that you'll have time for a little nap or a game of backgammon or a walk before your guests arrive. The recipes in this section can be multiplied according to the number of people you wish to serve and there is enough variety to suit various tastes.

MENU I
PLANNED FOR AN INDEFINITE NUMBER OF PEOPLE

Pheasant Pies   Steak and Kidney Pies   Veal and Ham Pies
Brandied Peaches   Watermelon Pickle   Brandied Crabapples
Preserved Kumquats   Cauliflower Gratinées
Jellied Watercress Rings Circled with Bibb Lettuce
filled with
Roquefort Yogurt, Hearts of Palm, Small Tomatoes and Capers
Brie Brûlé   Chocolate Cake Rolls with Chestnut Butter
Plateau des Fruits
with
Pears, Bing Cherries, Green Figs, Apricots
Plateau des Fromages
with
Chèvre, Brillat Savarin, Reblochon, Camembert
Biscuits

With the pies serve a variety of hearty red wines, Côte du Rhône, a California Pinot Noir, and a good Rioja. If you feel so inclined, serve champagne with the desserts, and a choice of port or Madeira with the cheeses.

PHEASANT PIE

SERVES 10

This is a recipe of Steven Connell, an inventive and gifted young chef-caterer who knows how to amuse New York's most knowing palates. For the last 5 years, he has also been my very close friend. I couldn't get along without him.

*Pie Dough for an 8-inch round or a 7 × 10-inch oblong dish (recipe
    follows)*
2 (4-pound) pheasants
1 carrot, sliced
1 onion, sliced
1 stalk celery, sliced
1 bay leaf
salt
6 peppercorns

Cut up the pheasants and parboil with the other ingredients for ½ hour in
water to cover. Remove, reserving the broth. Bone the meat in chunks, discarding skin and bones.

8 medium potatoes
1 pound white mushrooms
4 tablespoons butter

Peel, clean and quarter the potatoes and set aside. Sauté the mushrooms
briefly in the butter and set aside.

about 1 tablespoon cornstarch
¼ cup sherry

Strain the pheasant stock and reduce it by half (you will have about 2½
cups); thicken with cornstarch to medium-thick consistency. Add sherry
and season to taste. Arrange the pheasant meat, the potatoes (uncooked)
and the mushrooms in a shallow gratinée dish about 8 inches round or a
7 × 10-inch oblong. Pour the sauce over the dish.

Roll the crust to fit and cover the pie. Gash the crust and trim it with
pastry cut-outs, brush with egg wash (made by mixing 1 egg with 1 tablespoon milk) and bake the pie for 1 hour in a 350° F. oven. The potatoes
will be cooked through, absorbing and thickening the sauce. The tastes are
simply delicious.

PIE DOUGH

1 BIG PIE CRUST

1¾ cups flour
1 tablespoon salt
⅔ cup Crisco
⅓ cup ice water

Put flour, salt and Crisco in a processor. Process until crumbly. Add the ice water. Process for a few seconds longer until the dough gathers into a ball. Remove and chill in the refrigerator.

STEAK AND KIDNEY PIE

SERVES 8–10

½ pound mushrooms
½ stick butter
2½ pounds lean beef (top round or sirloin tip) cut in cubes
1 pound veal kidneys or, if not available, lamb kidneys, cut in pieces
½ cup seasoned flour
1 glass good red wine
¾ pound carrots, scraped and cut in large pieces
2 packages small frozen onions
salt and black pepper to taste
1 clove garlic, crushed
fresh parsley or other fresh or dried herbs
watercress pastry for pie crust*

* Simply add ⅓ bunch finely chopped watercress leaves to Pie Dough recipe (see Index).

Preheat oven to 350° F.

Slice the mushrooms coarsely and cook briefly in part of the butter. Set aside. Dredge the meat in the seasoned flour and brown in the same pan. When the meats are brown add the wine, cover the pan and cook over very low heat until tender. This will probably take about ½ hour. Meanwhile cook the carrots and onions (the frozen ones are very good and save time and tears) until just barely tender. Add some of the vegetable water to the meat pan and stir to make a smooth sauce. Season with salt, pepper, crushed garlic and fresh or dried herbs to taste. Combine the meat and vegetables in a 1½-quart casserole and cover with pastry. Brush with egg wash made by mixing 1 egg with 1 tablespoon milk. Watercress pastry is very good on this pie. Fifty minutes before you are ready to eat the pie put it in the oven.

This recipe may be made in multiples of 2, 3 or 4 for large groups.

VEAL AND HAM PIE

SERVES 10

2½ pounds veal
1½ pounds sliced ham
2 tablespoons flour
salt, black pepper and cayenne pepper to taste
grated rind of 1 lemon
chopped fresh herbs as available and to taste
10 artichoke hearts
½ cup beef stock
1 recipe Pie Dough (see Index)

Preheat oven to 350° F.

Remove all fat from meats and cut into thin slices. Mix flour and seasonings and roll each piece of veal in the mixture. Fill a casserole with alternate layers of veal and ham, mixing in the herbs, and top with the artichoke hearts. (Tinned artichoke hearts are very delicate.) Add the beef stock, cover with pastry and decorate the crust with pastry cut-outs; slash well and bake 1¼ hours.

WATERCRESS RING

1 (6-CUP) MOLD

4 cups chicken broth·
2 shallots, chopped
3 bunches watercress leaves (remove the thick stems)
3½ tablespoons gelatin
juice of 2 lemons

Place 2 cups of the chicken broth, the shallots and the watercress in a blender or processor and turn on for ½ minute. Soften the gelatin in ½ cup of the chicken broth; add to remaining 1½ cups chicken broth and heat until dissolved. Combine the mixtures, add the lemon juice and pour into an oiled mold. Refrigerate until firm.

CHOCOLATE CAKE ROLL

SERVES 8

This recipe is from *Entertaining Is an Art*, published by the Art Museum Council, Los Angeles County Museum of Art.

7 eggs, separated
¾ cup sugar
7 ounces dark sweet chocolate
6 tablespoons liquid coffee
bitter cocoa
2 pints heavy cream, whipped

Beat the egg yolks until they are very thick. Add the sugar gradually, beating constantly. Continue beating until the mixture is thick and very heavy. Break the chocolate into pieces and melt in the coffee. Stir until the mixture is smooth; allow it to cool for a moment and then blend the chocolate with the sugar-egg mixture. Fold in the stiffly beaten egg whites.

Line a cookie sheet with waxed paper after greasing with vegetable shortening. Grease the waxed paper with vegetable shortening. Pour the batter onto the cookie sheet and bake the roll for 10 minutes in the oven. Turn off the heat and allow the roll to remain in the oven for about 5 minutes, until it tests done. Remove from the oven and cover the surface of the roll immediately with a towel that has been wrung out in cold water. Place at once in the refrigerator to cool. When the bottom of the pan is cool, remove the towel and sprinkle bitter cocoa all over the surface of the cake, using a strainer and a teaspoon. Turn the roll out onto overlapping pieces of waxed paper. Carefully remove the paper stuck to the bottom of the roll and spread the surface with plain whipped cream. Roll up and dust with more cocoa.

BRIE BRÛLÉ

24 SMALL SERVINGS

*1 (8-inch) round Brie (24 ounces), not fully ripened, top rind
    removed*
1 cup chopped pecans
2 cups firmly packed brown sugar
crackers

Preheat broiler.

Place Brie in 10-inch quiche dish or pie plate and sprinkle with nuts. Cover top and sides with sugar, patting gently with fingertips. Broil on lowest rack until sugar bubbles and melts, about 3 minutes (cheese should retain its shape). Serve immediately with crackers.

MENU II

Curry of Chicken   *Curry of Shrimp*   *Curry of Lamb*

Popadums   *Mango Chutney*   *Rice*
Preserved Kumquats   *"Boys"*   *Cucumber Yogurt with Fresh Mint*
Green Salad

Poires en Croûte with Caramel Sauce (see Index)
Délice d'Abricots with Chocolate Sauce (see Index)
Brie Brûlé (see Index)   *Chocolate Leaf Cookies*

Accompanied by
Plateau des Fruits, Persimmons, Purple Grapes,
Papayas, Green Grapes, Melons, Garnished with Mint,
Lemon Halves and Lime Halves

A choice of Rhine wines, several dry Bordeaux and beers

The little bowls of condiments that accompany the serving of a fine curry party are called "boys" because, in the halcyon days of the empire, they were presented in splendid procession, a different boy passing each of the many condiments. Among those that you may choose to consider are, besides the hot chutney and the cool contrast of cucumbers in yogurt, some of the following:

Freshly grated coconut, a heaping bowl of it
Grated orange rind   *Grated green pepper*
Crumbled crisp hot bacon   *Chopped roasted peanuts*
Chopped hard-boiled egg whites   *Chopped hard-boiled egg yolks*
Raisins plumped in rum
Bananas fried in brown sugar and lemon juice
Chopped candied ginger
Bombay duck (available in specialty food stores)
Chopped candied pineapple   *Chopped sweet onion*

These three curry recipes are a little time-consuming but are fun to make and, as the flavor increases in blending together, they should be made ahead of time. The spices are best when prepared at home from the whole products.

Because they are planned for a large party here, I have not used as much garlic as I'd otherwise tend to and have added a little flour to thicken the sauce. These are large recipes so I will give them in stages. Very tasty, indeed. Serve piping hot with white rice.

CHICKEN CURRY

4 chickens, about 3 pounds each, quartered
1 pair chicken breasts
4 medium onions, quartered
2 carrots, cut in chunks
4 stalks celery, sliced
4 bay leaves
2 sprigs parsley
2 tablespoons salt
1 teaspoon whole black peppercorns

Place the above ingredients in a large kettle with water to cover and bring just to the boil. Simmer until chicken is cooked, about 20 minutes more. Remove the chicken pieces and cool them. Set aside the stock.

1½ sticks butter
3 cups chopped onions
2 large apples, peeled, cored and chopped
4 cloves garlic, crushed

Cook together over low heat until the onions and apples become mushy soft, about 15–20 minutes.

When the stock has cooled, strain and skim it. You will have about 5 quarts good homemade chicken stock. (Some will be used in the two following recipes.)

½ cup flour
1½ quarts chicken stock
2 teaspoons ground ginger
2 teaspoons ground turmeric
½ teaspoon ground cloves
2 teaspoons ground coriander
2 teaspoons ground cumin
1 teaspoon ground cinnamon
2 tablespoons good commercial curry powder
1 cup Coconut Cream (see NOTE)
1 jigger sweet sherry

Add the flour to the onion-apple mixture and gradually stir in the chicken stock. Add the spices and allow to cook over lowest heat for ½ hour or so. Stir in the coconut cream and sherry.

Meanwhile, skin and bone the chicken and divide it into rather large pieces. Add the chicken to the curry sauce and set aside until serving time.

NOTE To make Coconut Cream, combine ¼ cup fresh coconut pieces in a food processor equipped with the steel blade with 1 scant cup milk and whirl until milky.

CURRIED SHRIMP

ABOUT 15 SERVINGS

In this recipe, I use curry somewhat lightly, with the intention of letting the delicate flavor of the shrimp prevail. Bamboo shoots add a nice contrast in texture.

1½ sticks butter
3 cups chopped onion
3 cloves garlic, crushed
2 pears, peeled, cored and chopped

Cook together over very low heat until the onion and pear become mushy soft, about 15 minutes.

½ cup flour
1½ cups chicken stock
2 teaspoons ground ginger
2 teaspoons ground coriander
1 teaspoon ground cinnamon
1½ tablespoons good commercial curry powder
1 cup Coconut Cream (see Index)
5 pounds raw shrimp
1 can sliced bamboo shoots, drained
1 jigger dry sherry
¼ cup minced dill for garnish

Peel and clean the shrimp. Place in salted boiling water. Immediately drain and cool. This, with the later reheating in their sauce, will cook them sufficiently.

Add the flour to the onion mixture and gradually stir in the chicken stock. Add the spices and allow to cook for ½ hour or so. Stir in the Coconut Cream, the shrimp, bamboo shoots and sherry and set aside until serving time. After reheating, garnish with the dill.

CURRIED LAMB

ABOUT 15 SERVINGS

1 (5–7-pound) roast leg of lamb au jus (see Index)

Cool the lamb and cut it into bite-size pieces. Skim and reserve the juices.

1½ sticks butter
3 cups chopped onion
2 large apples, peeled, cored and chopped
4 cloves garlic, crushed
grated zest of 1 lemon

Cook together over very low heat until the onions and apples become mushy soft, about 15 minutes.

½ cup flour
4 cloves garlic, crushed
1½ quarts chicken stock
the juices from the leg of lamb
2 teaspoons ground coriander
2 teaspoons ground cumin
1 teaspoon ground cinnamon
2 tablespoons good commercial curry powder
2 teaspoons ground turmeric
½ teaspoon ground cloves
1 teaspoon poppyseeds
1 jigger sweet sherry
1 cup Coconut Cream (see Index)

Add the flour, spices, sherry and Coconut Cream to the onion-apple mixture. Gradually stir in the chicken stock and the juices from the leg of lamb and cook over low heat for ½ hour or so. Add the cut-up lamb to the sauce and set aside until serving time.

WHITE RICE

SERVES 45

Rice may be cooked by this method in the morning, set aside and reheated at night. It will be perfectly fluffy.

boiling water
3 tablespoons salt
2 tablespoons vegetable oil
3 pounds white rice

Fill a 4-gallon stockpot with water and bring to the boil. Add the salt, vegetable oil and rice. Bring again to the boil; stir once so the rice does not stick to the bottom of the pot and boil, covered, for 16 minutes. Drain.

Rinse in cold water to stop the cooking and set aside. Before serving, reheat the covered pot of rice in a 275° F. oven.

An English Picnic

Ivy Hall in Piscataway, New Jersey, is a fine stone manor house built in the days when our country was still an English colony. It stands strong and foursquare above the Raritan River. For years, Ivy Hall was the country house of Mr. and Mrs. Stephen Van Rensselaer Strong. It is now Ivy Hall Museum held in the public trust.

On the occasion of its passing from the Strong Estate to the State of New Jersey, Mrs. Strong, my good friend Mimi, decided to give it a smashing farewell. Tents to the left of us, tents to the right of us (bivouacs for the newly formed Friends of Ivy Hall, and the venerable House of Christie's, which was auctioning off some of the contents of the place).

We planned for this June day a nice relaxed English picnic under our own yellow-and-white striped tent between the garden of pink peonies and the aquamarine coolness of the swimming pool.

I think there were 75–100 there; of course, we didn't count but the menu seemed a lot of fun and the guests were amused.

We felt that on the whole it was adequate to the fact that Lord Cornwallis, too, had once lived at Ivy Hall. This is the picnic we served.

MENU III

Cold Sliced Tongue on Boston Lettuce
Cold Smoked Sliced Chicken on Boston Lettuce
Cold Whole York Ham

English Mustard Sauce   Mayonnaise with Fresh Herbs

Bangers Braised in Beer

Hot Country Bread   Molds of Sweet Butter
Hot New Potato Salad with Herbs and Bacon
Quail Eggs   Zucchini Slaw
Crisp Cucumber Aspic with Farmer Cheese Dressing
Cold New Peas with Mint

The Magnificent Nine

Cheddar   Double Gloucester   Cheshire   Sage Derby   Stilton
Wensleydale   Leicester   Caerphilly   Lancashire

Walnuts   Golden Apples   Port
English Trifle with Sauce Anglaise
Strawberries with Devonshire Cream

Ginger Beer, Beer, Stout and Champagne

BANGERS BRAISED IN BEER

SERVES ABOUT 40 WITH OTHER DISHES

A standby of England's working people, these pork sausages are marvelous for a big picnic crowd. Mustard, Branston pickle chutney and Cheddar cheese bring bangers extra zing.* They are not expensive and a great change from hot dogs.

5 pounds bangers
1 (12-ounce) can beer or ale

* Bangers are available in New York City at the Navaho Market, 1665 First Avenue, in 5-pound boxes.

Arrange the bangers in the beer in big open roasting pans and place them in a 350° F. oven, turning them from time to time until the beer is absorbed and the bangers are brown all over. Serve hot.

HOT NEW POTATO SALAD WITH HERBS AND BACON

SERVES 20

4 pounds small new potatoes
4 hard-boiled eggs
½ pound lean bacon
2 cloves garlic, mashed
½ cup finely chopped shallots
2 tablespoons finely chopped fresh dill
2 tablespoons finely chopped fresh chives
2 tablespoons finely chopped fresh parsley
1 tablespoon finely chopped fresh tarragon, or 1 teaspoon dried
¼ cup dry white wine
vegetable oil
salt and freshly ground black pepper to taste
garden lettuce
capers

Wash the potatoes and put in a kettle. Add cold water to cover and salt to taste. Bring to a boil and cook until tender, 15–20 minutes. At the same time hard-cook the eggs and fry the bacon until crisp. Drain on paper towels. Drain the potatoes, peel and slice the eggs. Slice the potatoes and mix with the garlic, shallots and herbs; add the sliced eggs and toss with the white wine and oil, salt and pepper. Toss the lettuce in oil, arrange in a salad bowl and spoon in the potato salad. Garnish with crumbled bacon and capers and serve while still warm.

ZUCCHINI SLAW

Here is an offbeat salad, subtle in flavor and quickly prepared. It is delicate and not expensive, a real blessing for big parties.

2 pounds zucchini
1 cup dill mayonnaise
salt and white pepper to taste
lettuce leaves
Walnut Oil Dressing (recipe follows)
grated orange rind for garnish
tomato and cucumber slices (optional)

Wash, dry and trim the zucchini; cut in 2-inch sections and run it through the shredding disc of a food processor. Mix with about 1 cup dill mayonnaise; add salt and white pepper. Set aside.

At serving time, pile the zucchini on a bed of tender lettuce leaves which have been tossed until coated in Walnut Oil Dressing. Garnish with grated orange rind and surround with thinly sliced tomatoes and cucumbers, if desired. (These are quickly prepared with a food slicer.)

WALNUT OIL DRESSING

½ CUP

6 tablespoons walnut oil
2 tablespoons white wine vinegar
¾ teaspoon salt
freshly ground black pepper
½ clove garlic, crushed (optional)

Combine all ingredients, mix thoroughly and chill. Mix again before using.

CRISP CUCUMBER ASPIC

Mrs. Griswold Frelinghuysen, of Woodstock, Vermont, perfected this appetizing summer dish.

4 thin cucumbers (2 peeled, 2 unpeeled)
4 tender stalks celery, minced
1 green pepper, minced
2 tablespoons grated onion
chopped herbs (dill, chives and/or parsley, as available)
2 teaspoons salt
2 tablespoons sugar
½ cup lemon juice
½ cup lemon vinegar
4 packages gelatin, softened in 1 cup cold water
4 cups boiling water
4–6 drops green food coloring
Farmer Cheese Dressing (recipe follows)

Slice the seedless end parts of the cucumbers, using about half of each. Then remove the seeds from the center sections and dice them. Mix together all of the vegetables and the cucumber slices. Add the seasonings and, lastly, the gelatin softened in water, the boiling water and the food coloring. Pour into a 2-quart mold and chill until set. Serve on a bed of greens with Farmer Cheese Dressing.

FARMER CHEESE DRESSING

1 cup farmer cheese
1 cup sour cream
2 tablespoons horseradish
2 tablespoons capers

Mix all together and chill before serving.

THE MAGNIFICENT NINE

The variety of English cheeses is less well known to most of us than that of France, but with her rich milk-producing counties, England has developed many. The leading favorites are known to Britons, who are real cheese lovers, as the Magnificent Nine. For the English, cheese can be a meal. Every pub, whether in the countryside or in London, serves a "plough-man's lunch," a robust and satisfying repast which consists, quite simply, of a fine hunk of Cheddar, generous pieces of good bread, a pickle or two and fresh butter, though purists demur at the butter and declare stoutly that only a bad cheese needs butter. This is, of course, a matter of taste, but I like buttered bread. Wash the meal down with a pint of ale and the inner man is happily satisfied.

Cheddar is so well loved that its name is almost synonymous with "cheese" to many people both there and in other English-speaking nations. It originally ripened in the damp caves of the Cheddar Gorge in Somerset in the fifteenth century.

Older yet in history, known as far back as the twelfth century, is *Cheshire* cheese. Light in color, firm in texture, creamy and slightly salty to the taste, it is celebrated by the old and renowned pub in Fleet Street that bears its name and, like Cheddar, it goes best with beer.

Double Gloucester is firm, orange and full of taste. At one time, Gloucester came in two strengths, but the stronger variety outran single Gloucester in popularity until production of the latter ceased. Double Gloucester is a fine end-of-a-meal cheese, excellent for slicing for sandwiches, excellent for rarebits.

Derby (pronounced Darby, of course) is pale in color and of fine texture. At Christmastime and at harvest it was traditional to add the juice of pulped sage and spinach leaves and this attractive cheese, *Sage Derby*, became so popular that it is now available all year round. Light and veined with green, it looks like pale malachite, a beautiful addition to the cheese tray.

Delicately rainbow-hued *Stilton*, moist, melting, crumbly and rich, is England's pride. Sometimes drenched with port, it is better savored with a fine glass of that wine to accompany it, a cheese that is worthy of full attention whenever it is available. A big wedge from a ripe Stilton cheese is a holiday feast. Crack walnuts with it for perfect bliss.

Wensleydale, also rich, but light and crumbly, almost rivals Stilton in popularity. If you have not tried it, do. You will find it a delight with a crisp slice of apple.

Leicester (say "Lester") and pale *Caerphilly* from Wales are ideal dessert cheeses. *Lancashire* cheese is somewhat harder to find in our shops but is worth tracking down to get to know all of England's Magnificent Nine.

ENGLISH TRIFLE

30 OR MORE SERVINGS

The recipe for this trifle is reconstructed from fond memory of the ones we used to love at the Connaught in London. The Connaught, in an atmosphere of comfortable opulence, serves perhaps the finest cuisine in Britain, and certainly theirs is the most irresistible trifle ever to be imagined.

Sauce Anglaise (recipe follows)
1 pound ladyfingers or pound cake cut in finger-sized strips
¾ cup slivered almonds (an equal quantity of sliced English walnuts
*   makes a splendid alternative)*
7 egg whites, beaten until stiff with ¼ cup sugar
1 (12-ounce) jar of jam, damson plum, blackberry or gooseberry
1 pint heavy cream, whipped and sweetened to taste

Prepare the Sauce Anglaise and, while it is cooling, line a large bowl with ladyfingers or strips of pound cake.

Add the almonds to the Sauce Anglaise, reserving a few to garnish the final dish.

Beat the egg whites and sugar and fold into the cooled Sauce Anglaise, amalgamating them only partially. Pour the mixture into the center of the cake-lined bowl. Cover with big dollops of the jam, amalgamating this, too, lightly with the sauce. Cover with dollops of whipped cream or pipe the cream over the dessert with a pastry tube. Chill for several hours and serve garnished with the reserved almond slivers.

SAUCE ANGLAISE
English Custard

7 egg yolks
1 cup sugar
3 cups milk
⅓ teaspoon salt
2 tablespoons kirsch or, traditionally, sherry

Place the yolks in a large, heavy-bottomed saucepan and add the sugar, whisking until thick and lemon-colored.

Meanwhile, bring the milk nearly to the boiling point.

Whisking constantly, gradually add the hot milk to the sugar-and-yolk mixture. Add the salt. Using a wooden spoon, begin stirring, making certain the spoon touches the entire bottom of the pan so that no sticking or burning occurs.

Cook until the mixture has a custardlike quality, at which point it will coat the spoon. Be careful that the sauce does not boil or it will curdle. Now set the custard in a basin of cold water. Let it cool to room temperature. Stir in the kirsch or sherry and refrigerate for 1 hour or longer.

A Midnight Supper

A menu for a dinner dance or after-theater supper

For a number of years, we used to have a costume dance on St. Valentine's Day. People came dressed as famous lovers of fact and fiction and the variety of ideas that people dreamed up was highly entertaining. We danced till dawn.

These are dishes that appeared from time to time at those parties, light but sustaining things for midnight appetites.

Arrange them on a large buffet or dining room table centered lavishly with fruits and flowers, champagne bottles in silver buckets and 3 chafing dishes.

MENU IV

PLANNED FOR AN INDEFINITE NUMBER

A Whole Smoked Salmon

Filet de Boeuf au Jus

in chafing dishes:
Creamed Oysters   Lobster in Champagne Sauce
Fettucini and Mushrooms on Toast Points
Egg Mousse on Lettuce Leaves
Endive Salad   Wild Rice Salad
Hot Buttered Herbed French Bread Fingers

Baskets of Fruit   Fresh Almonds
. . . . and a tray of cheeses including a triple-crème, L'Explorateur,
with Bar-le-Duc to eat with it.

Canteloupe Ice in Canteloupe Rings
Angel Food Cake   Candies   Preferitos

Serve champagne throughout

LOBSTER IN CHAMPAGNE SAUCE

For presenting in the chafing dish, prepare this lobster dish in advance in the kitchen. Just before serving, fill the chafing dish and keep the lobster hot there. This quantity should be enough to refill the chafing dish twice.

1 stick butter
1 small onion, minced
½ cup flour
1 cup milk
seasoning to taste:
   salt
   cayenne
   chopped fresh dill
   fresh or dried tarragon
1 cup heavy cream
1 cup champagne
2 eggs, beaten
4 pounds lobster meat (cooked)

Melt the butter over low heat and cook the onion until soft. Add the flour and gradually stir in the milk and seasoning; cook gently for 2–3 minutes, stirring. Stir in the heavy cream, champagne and eggs and cook together for a minute longer without boiling. Add the lobster meat and set aside. Reheat before transferring to the chafing dish.

EGG MOUSSE ON LETTUCE LEAVES

SERVES 8–10

This is a favorite dish of Mrs. William Gubelmann of Henley-on-Thames, England. It's very versatile.

10 hard-boiled eggs
¾ cup heavy cream, whipped
½ cup mayonnaise
Worcestershire sauce, to taste
1 cup jellying consommé (reserve ½ cup; see below)
1 envelope gelatin, softened in 2 tablespoons cold water
capers (optional), if caviar isn't used to garnish the dish
salt and pepper to taste
lettuce leaves
5 or 6 slices cooked, crisp, crumbled bacon or lumpfish caviar for
* garnish*

Dice the eggs fine and add the cream, mayonnaise, Worcestershire sauce, consommé, gelatin mixture and capers, if used, plus the seasonings. Chill in refrigerator for a couple of hours in an attractive metal mold.

Pour the reserved consommé atop the mold and chill to set. After unmolding (using a brief dip in hot water, if necessary) turn onto a serving dish on a bed of lettuce leaves and sprinkle with a garnish of crumpled crisp bacon or lumpfish caviar.

This dish can be chilled overnight, omitting the final arrangement and garnishing until ready to serve.

HOT BUTTERED HERBED FRENCH
BREAD FINGERS

32 PIECES

2 loaves French bread
1½ sticks butter
finely minced fresh herbs, as available
1 small clove crushed garlic (optional)

Preheat oven to 300° F.

Quarter each loaf of bread by slitting in half from end to end, once hori-
zontally, then again vertically. Cut crosswise 3 times, making "fingers."
Melt the butter; add minced herbs and garlic if used and brush the cut sur-
faces of the bread with the mixture. Place on baking sheets, cut edges up,
and heat for 5 minutes. Serve hot in napkin-lined baskets.

WILD RICE SALAD

3 QUARTS

4 cups cooked wild rice (see Index)
4 cups cooked chick-peas
2 cups white seedless grapes
2 cups pecans, coarsely chopped
1 cup peanut oil
⅓ cup raspberry vinegar
salt and freshly ground pink pepper to taste

Mix all ingredients together and serve at room temperature.

PREFERITOS (CUBAN)

The recipe of Mrs. Stephen Sanford's Cuban chef, these cookies are intriguing in texture and flavor. From her kitchen emanate not only the spicy odors of his cooking, but also the soft rhythms of rhumba music, for Manolo is the favorite dancing master of *tout* Palm Beach and merrymakers gather there to the clicking of castanets to turn the kitchen into a make-believe ballroom.

Because they are light, preferitos are ideal for large parties and teas. Remember, don't try to make meringues on a rainy day. (These cookies are similar to the cinnamon stars of old-fashioned Christmases and can be cut with a star cutter at holiday time and stored in tins.)

½ pound butter (2 sticks)
1¼ cups sugar
1 pound almonds, grated
2 ounces water
1 tablespoon vanilla extract
6 eggs, separated
3¼ cups flour
1 teaspoon cinnamon

Preheat oven to 300° F.

In a mixing bowl, cream together the butter and 1 cup of the sugar. Stir in ½ pound of the grated almonds. In a separate bowl, mix water, vanilla extract and egg yolks. Add this, with the flour, to the butter mixture and work into a pastry. Roll it very thinly on a floured pastry board. Cut into diamond shapes and place on a cookie sheet.

Beat egg whites till stiff and fold in the remaining sugar and almonds and the cinnamon. Spread pastry diamonds with this meringue mix and bake for approximately 25 minutes.

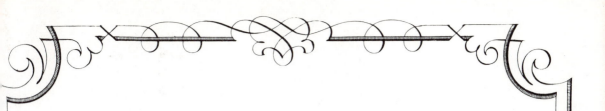

HOLIDAYS GREAT AND SMALL

Great holidays bring out the innate sense of hospitality in everyone of us and the man or woman who takes special pleasure in entertaining is imbued at holiday time with a fervor to rise once again to the joyful opportunity. In casting back over these happy times, I think I cannot remember a single Thanksgiving dinner when the company didn't sigh happily as the feast ended and say, "This is the *best* Thanksgiving we have ever had." Oddly enough, each time it's true. Somehow, they just do get better and better!

Each year it's fun on these occasions to try to think of some amusing innovations to mingle with the dishes that tradition has led us to expect; each year a fine wine has been saved for the great day; each year the thoughtful guest secures some rare delicacy to complement the feast. Each year even the slenderest beauty throws caution to the wind and tucks in her napkin with no thought but that the feast's the thing!

The lesser holidays present added opportunity for added fun. For years, we had a Boxing Day party with dancing and light merriment. Everyone loved that carefree occasion on the day after Christmas. Once we had a Groundhog Day party to cheer us on the second day of February. All I can remember now is that the little creature, molded out of cheese and bristling with toothpicks, *did* see his shadow with the beady black olives that were his eyes. Kentucky Derby Day, Election Day . . . they all have their special flavor. I've included here ideas for 10 festive gatherings.

St. Valentine's Day

This romantic holiday is an ideal time to give a little love feast in the midst of winter's cold blasts, to use your pink or red tablecloth, place cards, menus, favors and arrangements of hearts and the flowers of spring, tulips, narcissi, carnations, anemones, camelias, freesia and lilies in a carefree mass.

Crab-Meat and Shrimp Soup Garnished with Red Caviar
Herbed Toasts
Roast Pheasant
Bread Sauce   Tabasco Jelly
Wild Rice (see Index)
Tiny Peas, Snow Peas and Cucumbers with Pimiento

Champagne Ice with Raspberries or Strawberries

There are occasions when it is festive to serve several wines. No more wine is consumed, but variety lends a great deal of interest to a party meal. The table looks exciting, set with several glasses. With this dinner, I would suggest serving sherry with the soup, a red Bordeaux with the pheasant, and Château d'Yquem with dessert will show them that you really care.

CRAB-MEAT AND SHRIMP SOUP GARNISHED WITH RED CAVIAR

SERVES 8

2 cans frozen shrimp bisque
1½ pints light cream
½ pound crab meat
1 jigger pale, dry sherry
red caviar for garnish
fresh tarragon leaves

Defrost the shrimp bisque and mix over low heat with the cream, crab meat and sherry. Store in the refrigerator. Serve in chilled soup plates garnished with red caviar and a few small sprigs of fresh tarragon.

HERBED TOASTS

parsley, tarragon and chives, to taste
½ cup soft butter
salt and pepper
1 thin loaf French bread

Preheat oven to 350° F.

Chop equal parts of parsley, tarragon and chives very fine and mix into soft butter. Add salt and pepper. Spread the butter on very thin slices of French bread. Toast in the oven until golden brown and crisp.

ROAST PHEASANT

Here is the very successful recipe of Princess Henry Reuss of Austria. She and her husband lead fabled lives, dividing their time among their four mountaintop wild game preserves. One is at Altenfelden in Upper Austria, one at Horn in Kitzbühl. Another is a thirteenth-century hunting lodge, Rosegg, in Corinthia, and finally there is Mautern in Styria. Prince Henry, who is president of the Conseil International de la Chasse, an ancient order devoted to the protection of hunted animals, has collected rare beasts from every corner of the world (preserving some from extinction) and naturalized them in his mountain Wildparks.

Venison, wild boar, chamois, game birds of every feather, but not the endangered species, of course, are everyday fare at their hospitable table. The princess, when visiting me toward the completion of this book, offered this as her favorite preparation for pheasant.

4 (2½–3-pound) pheasants
salt and freshly ground black pepper to taste
4 bay leaves
2 carrots, sliced
2 stalks celery, sliced
1 lemon, sliced
8 slices bacon
butter
2 jiggers cognac

Preheat oven to 350° F.

Sprinkle the pheasants inside and out with salt and pepper and place a bay leaf, some sliced carrots, celery and lemon in each. Tie the legs together with string and clip off the tips of the wings. Rub the pheasant with butter and pour a jigger of cognac over each. Place 2 strips bacon on each bird and cover the birds with a tent of aluminum foil. Roast, basting occasionally, until done, about 40 minutes.

BREAD SAUCE

2 cups milk
3 slices white bread
½ onion
6 cloves
1 teaspoon salt
a few grains cayenne pepper
3 tablespoons butter

Put the milk in the top of a double boiler. Break in the bread, from which the crusts have been removed, and set aside. Add the onion stuck with cloves and cook gently for 30 minutes. Remove and discard the clove-studded onion and beat the sauce until smooth, adding to it the salt, cayenne and 2 tablespoons of the butter. Make crumbs from some of the bread crusts and sauté in the remaining butter. Pour the sauce into a hot sauceboat and sprinkle with the browned crumbs.

TABASCO JELLY

1 GLASS

1 glass red currant jelly
1–2 teaspoons Tabasco sauce
1 teaspoon lemon juice

Melt the jelly in the top of a double boiler and season to taste with Tabasco. Add lemon juice. Remove from heat; chill in a small mold. Dip briefly in boiling water and unmold.

TINY PEAS, SNOW PEAS AND
CUCUMBERS WITH PIMIENTO

SERVES 8–10 (DEPENDING ON OTHER DISHES USED)

½ pound snow peas, sliced diagonally into ⅛-inch pieces
1 large cucumber
3 cups small fresh peas
3 tablespoons sweet butter
salt, freshly ground white pepper and parsley to taste
½ canned pimiento, cut into small diamonds

Slice the snow peas. Peel and halve the cucumber, remove the seeds and, with a small melon-ball cutter, cut balls of cucumber. Cook the first 3 vegetables in 1 cup boiling salted water until just tender, 3–5 minutes. Drain them, add the butter and toss with salt, pepper and parlsey to taste. Turn into a heated serving dish and garnish with pimiento.

CHAMPAGNE ICE

A recipe of Mrs. Frank McMahon, an accomplished hostess of Palm Beach and Bermuda.

2 cups water
2 cups sugar
2 tablespoons grated lemon rind
½ cup lemon juice
¼ cup white corn syrup
1 bottle domestic champagne
1 pint fresh strawberries, sliced, or fresh whole raspberries
Grand Marnier
confectioners' sugar

Boil water and sugar until sugar dissolves. Add grated lemon rind, juice and corn syrup. Let cool and stir in champagne. This mixture should be frozen in a freezer using traditional methods. Freezing requires considerable time as it contains alcohol. Keep in deep freeze; mix occasionally with a dinner fork while in freezer.

Serve topped with fresh strawberries or raspberries dipped in Grand Marnier and confectioners' sugar.

Mardi Gras Dinner

FOR 8

Cream of Almond Soup
Cheese Straws (see Index)

Lobster Carnaval
Potatoes Allumette
Légumes Pavés

Profiteroles au Chocolat, Pistachio Nuts (see Index)

Café Diable flamed in the chafing dish

Champagne

CREAM OF ALMOND SOUP

SERVES 8–10

2 cups blanched almonds
3 tablespoons butter
1 small onion, sliced
1 stalk celery, sliced
3 tablespoons flour
2½ quarts chicken broth
1 teaspoon salt
½ teaspoon freshly ground white pepper
cayenne pepper
1 cup light cream
1 teaspoon almond extract
salted whipped cream (optional)
chopped chervil, tarragon or chives (optional)

Sliver about 30 of the almonds for garnish and toast them in a slow oven (260° F.). Crush the rest of the almonds in a food processor or a blender. Melt the butter in a soup kettle, add the onion and celery and cook slowly until soft but not brown. Add the flour and stir until smooth. Slowly add the broth, then the crushed almonds, salt, white pepper and a little cayenne pepper. Cook, stirring constantly, until the mixture comes to the boil. Turn heat very low and simmer for ½ hour, stirring occasionally. Purée by batches in the processor or blender and add the cream and almond extract. Serve hot or chilled, garnished with the toasted almonds and if you wish salted whipped cream and chopped chervil, tarragon or chives.

LOBSTER CARNAVAL

SERVES 8

8 live lobsters
salt and pepper
butter
Béchamel Sauce (see Index), *made with light cream, about 4 cups*
pinch dry mustard
1 cup grated Swiss cheese

Have the fishmonger split the lobsters in half lengthwise for broiling. Wash under running water to remove the head, sand sac and intestinal vein. Salt and pepper the interior, dot with butter and broil under a not-too-hot fire for about 15 minutes. Crack the claws, remove the meat and the shell meat and slice it. In the bottom of the two shells put a layer of Béchamel Sauce heightened with a little mustard. Fill the shell with lobster meat, cover with more sauce, sprinkle with grated Swiss cheese and brown in the oven before serving.

SERVES 8–10

10 large potatoes
fat
salt to taste

Peel and thoroughly dry potatoes with a towel. Cut them to make sticks about 2½ inches long and as thick as a wooden match. Fry in deep fat at 375° F., as for French-fried potatoes, for 4–5 minutes, until the potatoes are deep brown and crisp. Drain in paper towels, sprinkle with salt and serve at once.

LÉGUMES PAVÉS
The Purée of Four Vegetables, Served Together

SERVES 6–10

Select 4 vegetables of contrasting colors: broccoli, cauliflower, carrots and summer squash; or spinach, potatoes, winter squash and peas make good combinations. Cook each vegetable separately, reserving a few flowerets of broccoli, some julienne strips of carrot or some peas to decorate the final dish.

Purée each vegetable, seasoning each with a different spice or herb. Blend in butter or cream to achieve a good consistency.

Spoon each vegetable neatly into one quarter of a hot serving dish. Arrange a border of lightly steamed broccoli flowerets, julienne strips of carrot or peas to divide the vegetables.

4 tablespoons Coleman's mustard
1 cup dark-brown sugar
1 teaspoon ground cloves
1 teaspoon ground allspice
1 teaspoon ground ginger
1 cup ginger ale
1 cup orange juice
1 cup sherry
whole cloves (optional)
parsley for garnish
a paper frill for garnish

Preheat oven to 375° F.

Make a paste of the mustard, sugar, spices and some of the liquids. Remove the ham to a large roasting pan and skin it. It is a matter of preference in the South whether or not to score the surface of the ham lightly in a diamond pattern and stud it with cloves. Some cooks do so, while others feel that the ham needs no such adornment. Bake for 45 minutes under a tent made of heavy duty aluminum foil. During this cooking period the ham should be basted every 5 or 10 minutes with the remaining liquids and the pan juices. Remove the ham to a warm platter and garnish it with parsley and a paper frill.

PAPER FRILLS

The shank of a ham or leg of lamb or the drumstick of a turkey can easily be finished with a paper frill which will lend the roast or joint the élan which is its due. Lamb chops and chickens too look more splendid wearing these fine frills to a party.

Fold in half a piece of stiff parchment paper 12 × 12 inches (smaller, of course, for a chop or a bird), but do not press the crease. Cut the fold at ⅛–½-inch intervals (depending on the size of the frill) to within an inch of the open edge. Reverse the fold to give a puffed effect and bring the edges together again. Tie securely to the bone with white kitchen string.

CUMBERLAND SAUCE II

This, like the preceding recipe, was given me by Martin Shallenberger. He is now a world citizen but was born a Kentuckian, also born a cook!

1 glass currant jelly
½ cup ham glaze
1 teaspoon dry mustard
1 jigger Madeira
1 California orange

Melt the jelly and stir in the next 3 ingredients. Remove the zest from the orange; cut into hair-thin strips and reserve. Squeeze the orange juice and add to the sauce. Last, add the zest. Serve hot or cold.

SOUTHERN MUSTARD RABBIT

SERVES 8 OR MORE

2 rabbits (3½–4 pounds each)
flour
6 tablespoons butter
3 tablespoons olive oil
Dijon or herbed mustard
1 medium onion, finely chopped
1 cup sliced mushrooms
3 tablespoons chopped parsley
salt
freshly ground pepper
1 cup heavy cream
lemon juice (optional)

Preheat oven to 350° F.

Clean rabbits and cut into serving-size portions. Dry pieces and dredge in flour. Sauté in butter and olive oil in a heavy skillet until browned on all sides. Remove and spread pieces liberally with mustard. Place pieces in a shallow baking dish.

Sauté onion in fat remaining in skillet. Add mushrooms and continue cooking. Add parsley, salt and pepper to taste. Blend in cream and heat through. Pour mixture over rabbit and bake for 30–40 minutes. Correct seasoning as required. Add a few drops of lemon juice, if desired, and serve immediately.

SPOON BREAD

2–2½ QUART CASSEROLE

1½ cups cornmeal
1½ teaspoons salt
1½ tablespoons sugar
3 tablespoons butter
1½ cups water
3 cups buttermilk
5 eggs, well beaten

Preheat oven to 325° F.

Combine cornmeal, salt, sugar, butter, water and half the buttermilk in a saucepan. Cook over medium heat, stirring constantly, until the mixture thickens. Cool to room temperature before adding eggs and remaining buttermilk. Pour batter into a hot greased 2–2½-quart baking dish. Bake approximately 45 minutes. Serve immediately with plenty of butter.

CREAM OF TARTAR BISCUITS

YIELDS 30–36

Make certain that the cream of tartar and baking soda are fresh; otherwise, these snowy white biscuits will not achieve maximum fluffiness. They can be made ahead, stored in the refrigerator and reheated just before serving (475° F. for just 5 minutes).

2½ cups flour
2 heaping teaspoons fresh cream of tartar
1 teaspoon salt
1 heaping teaspoon fresh baking soda
1½–2 cups heavy cream, as required

Preheat oven to 475° F.

Sift together the first 3 ingredients with 2 cups flour. Toss with a mixing spoon to distribute ingredients evenly. Stir in cream while mixing gently. Stop after adding 1 cup and check to see that the batter is thick, lumpy and of a very moist consistency. If not, add remaining cream gradually as needed. Do not overmix. Final mixture should be like thick, lumpy, sticky oatmeal. If too liquid, add the remaining flour. All this should be done quickly and lightly. The batter should not look dark or greasy.

Turn out batter onto a floured pastry board. Roll dough to coat all sides lightly. Flour a rolling pin and roll out dough to ½-inch thickness.

Cut out circles measuring 1¾–2 inches in diameter to form the biscuits. Place biscuits close together, not quite touching, on an ungreased cookie sheet or in a jellyroll pan. Scraps can be gathered together and rerolled.

Prick each biscuit once lightly in the center with a fork so they will lift a little and the biscuits will be light. Bake for 2 or 3 minutes, then reduce heat to 425° and continue baking for about 10 minutes, until one biscuit tests done when broken open. Serve while warm.

PECAN PIES

The recipe of Liz Sarfati, who, with her husband, Claude, owned the Huntting Inn in East Hampton. She is Kentucky-born and -bred and this is a family recipe. It makes 2 light and delicate pies.

6 large eggs
2 cups sugar
2 cups dark Karo corn syrup (1 bottle)
2 teaspoons vanilla extract
½ teaspoon salt
2 cups pecan meats (broken meats may be used)
2 (8- or 9-inch) Basic Pie Crusts (see Index)
1 pint heavy cream, whipped

Preheat oven to 425° F.

Beat the eggs till foamy. Add the sugar, syrup, vanilla extract and salt. Divide the filling into 2 bowls and add half of the nuts to each. Pour in the 2 pie shells and bake for 15 minutes. Lower the heat to 375° and bake for 30 minutes longer. Cool and, when ready to serve, drop the whipped cream lightly on the 2 pies.

KEY LIME PIE

The authentic Key Lime Pie has a creamy yellow interior and just the right tartness to make a light and devastating warm weather dessert.

8 eggs, separated
2 cans condensed milk
⅔ cup Key lime juice
2 Basic Pie Crusts (see Index)
4 additional egg whites
4 tablespoons sugar

Preheat oven to 350° F.

Beat the yolks of 8 eggs and the whites of 2 until thick. Add the condensed milk and beat again. Add the lime juice and beat until thick. Beat the 6 remaining egg whites until dry and fold into the mixture. Pour into a baked pie shell. Beat the 4 additional egg whites until they form stiff peaks. Beat in the sugar and spread on top of the pie. Bake until the meringue is golden. Chill before serving.

A Wedding

This menu, planned with Steven Connell and used at the wedding of my daughter, Lisa, to Dale Booher, seems to me to provide the pleasantest sort of refreshments for five o'clock, when it is too early to think of a sit-down party. A wedding reception is a very special affair, not an overgrown cocktail party, and loving care in planning the refreshments helps to make it so. These suggestions may be followed for an indefinite number of guests.

Arrange to pass trays of champagne, punch, small sandwiches and small bites immediately upon the arrival of the wedding guests so that there is no awkward period of waiting. Later, provide heartier fare, a buffet and a variety of foods passed on trays. It is easier to arrange the menu so things can be eaten from a small plate with only a fork. More would be hard to manage.

The cutting and sharing of the wedding cake at the end of the reception is the high point of the party. Be sure to find one that tastes as good as it promises. With this wedding in April, we chose to serve, to accompany the cake, mounds of whole, fresh strawberries with powdered sugar to dip them in. At another time of year, the choice of fruit might be different.

Upon arrival of the guests:

Champagne   Fruit Punch
Salted Almonds   Small Chicken Sandwiches
Carpaccio with Capers (see Index)   *Pâté de Foie Gras Sandwiches*
Stuffed Pullet Eggs with Caviar   Watercress Sandwiches

a seafood bar including:

Oysters, Clams, Shrimp and Scallops Seviche
served on
Beds of Ice and Decorated with Seaweed
Sauce Verte (see Index)   *Lemon Halves   Sauce Rouge*

a crêpe bar providing:

Crêpes
filled with
Curried Chicken, Crab meat or Lobster Newburg, Smoked Salmon

---

pass at intervals:

Fillet Mignon Cooked with Madeira on Toast   *Croques Monsieur*
Cold Stuffed Breast of Veal on Toast (see Index)   *Croques Madame*
Garlic Sausage en Brioche   *Croques Concombres*
Smoked Chicken Breast Stuffed with Pesto
Stuffed Prunes Wrapped in Bacon   *Fresh Figs Wrapped in Prosciutto*

The Wedding Cake
Mounds of Whole Fresh Strawberries, Confectioners' Sugar

SCALLOPS SEVICHE

These little delicacies, "cooked" by marinating in lemon and lime juice, retain all the zest and vigor of the sea. This recipe is given for a buffet serving, but the dish lends itself to subdivision as a first course at either luncheon or dinner or for a before-dinner cocktail bite.

2 pounds bay scallops
juice of one lemon
juice of two limes
3 tablespoons onion juice
salt, grated ginger and freshly ground black pepper to taste
spinach leaves
oil
vinegar

Marinate the scallops in the juices and seasonings, starting the process the
day before you plan to serve them and stirring occasionally. Keep them
during this time in a covered dish in the refrigerator. At serving time drain
the scallops (reserving the lovely juice for something else—great for example, for Bloody Marys)—and serve on spinach leaves which have been
tossed in oil and vinegar.

SAUCE ROUGE

1 egg yolk at room temperature
1 teaspoon salt
½ teaspoon dry mustard
½ teaspoon paprika
2 tablespoons vinegar or lemon juice
1 cup fine olive or salad oil
1 ounce red caviar

Beat the egg yolk and dry seasonings thoroughly in a small bowl which has been rinsed with hot water and wiped dry. Add 1 tablespoon of the vinegar or lemon juice and beat again. Thoroughly beat in the oil, a few drops at a time, until ¼ cup is used, then add more oil rapidly, beating all the while. As the mixture thickens, add the remaining vinegar or lemon juice.

This may be made in an electric blender or food processor. Just be sure to add the oil slowly at first.

Just before serving, gently but thoroughly incorporate the red caviar into the sauce.

CROQUES

Croques Monsieur and Croques Madame are traditional French fare and are excellently adapted, cut small, for buffet service. Croques Concombre are, to the best of my knowledge, an American innovation, delicious *amuse-bouches*, served by Donald Bruce White and Steven Connell.

Have on hand enough good white bread, thinly sliced Gruyère cheese, ham, chicken and cucumbers to meet your requirements and proceed as follows:

FOR EACH 16 SMALL SANDWICHES

An egg wash made of:
  2 eggs
  1 cup milk
  salt and pepper to taste

Beat together.

FOR CROQUES MONSIEUR

8 slices bread
4 slices ham, to fit
8 slices Gruyère cheese, to fit
Dijon mustard
¼ pound butter, for sautéing

Assemble 4 large sandwiches. Dip both sides in egg wash and sauté in butter until golden on each side. Remove crusts with a sharp knife; cut into quarters and serve hot.

For Croques Madame, proceed in the same fashion, using sliced chicken instead of ham and finely cut chives instead of mustard.

For Croques Concombre, use unskinned, thinly sliced cucumbers with the Gruyère and Dijon mustard.

Election Day

Make this a party where a friendly and rather inelegant spirit prevails, something to suggest the atmosphere of an old New York Irish bar. For decorations use flags and red, white and blue streamers and posters of all the candidates. Plenty of eats are in order so the guests can pile up their own sandwiches.

Pretzels   *A Barrel of Beer*   *Liederkrantz*
Pickled Eggs   *Dill Pickles*

Cold Meats (Roast Beef, Pastrami, Ham), Cream Cheese, Lox
Rye Bread   *White Bread*   *Pumpernickel*
New England Baked Beans
Potato Salad   *Cole Slaw*   *Sauerkraut*   *Mustard*
Sliced Tomatoes
"21" Sauce   *Major Gray's Chutney*

And in two chafing dishes:
Creamed Oysters Americaine
Welsh Rarebit

Apple Pie
and
Ice-Cream Cones

NEW ENGLAND BAKED BEANS

Humble, heavenly, as far as I am concerned this is an irresistible dish. The recipe which I have evolved is more pungent than the original New England favorite; the shiny, mahogany-colored beans in their sweet-sour sauce are a nice surprise for an informal party.

2 pounds white marrow beans
4 large onions, chopped
salt
¾ cup black molasses
3 teaspoons salt
3 teaspoons dry mustard
3 teaspoons powdered ginger
4 cloves garlic, crushed
1 cup apple cider vinegar
1 pound salt pork
boiling water

Soak the beans overnight. Next morning parboil them in fresh water, salted, with the chopped onions until they are soft and a few of the skins start to break. Drain the beans.

Mix the remaining ingredients, except for the salt pork and boiling water, with the beans and place in a bean pot or brown earthenware casserole. Cut small pieces of salt pork and stir into the beans. Reserve 1 large piece, score it and press on top of the beans where it will brown. Cover with boiling water. Cover the pot and bake without stirring in a slow oven (250° F.) for 6 to 8 hours. Remove the pot's cover for the last hour of baking and replenish the boiling water if necessary. (Baked beans are at their best when cooked a day in advance, then reheated.)

COLE SLAW

1 large young head cabbage
2 red apples
1 cup heavy cream
1 clove garlic, crushed
5 tablespoons lemon vinegar
salt to taste
pinch celery seed
½ pound seedless grapes
1 bunch watercress

Remove the outside leaves and the tough part of the cabbage core and shred it fine in a food processor. Core and shred the apples (leaving the skin on them) and sprinkle with 2 tablespoons lemon vinegar. Wash and dry the watercress and, reserving a few sprigs for garnish, cut it fine.

Beat together the cream, garlic, about 3 tablespoons lemon vinegar, salt and celery seed until of the consistency of thin whipped cream. Mix the dressing with the shredded vegetables and the grapes and serve garnished with sprigs of watercress.

CREAMED OYSTERS AMERICAINE

1 quart shucked oysters
8 tablespoons butter
2 tablespoons grated onion
½ cup flour
3 cups milk
2 jiggers sherry or Madeira
2 eggs, lightly beaten
2 teaspoons salt
½ teaspoon freshly ground black pepper

Simmer the oysters in their liquor until the edges start to curl, 3–4 minutes. In a saucepan, melt the butter. Add the grated onion. With a wire whisk, stir in the flour. Add the milk, stirring vigorously with the wire whisk until thick and smooth. Whisk in the wine. Add the eggs, the oysters and their liquor, the salt and the pepper and cook over low heat until thick. Transfer to a chafing dish and serve.

Thanksgiving Day

---

with cocktails:
Venison Pâté with Pickled Walnuts
Hearts of Celery   Olives
Oysters on the Half Shell with Fresh Caviar

Roast Turkey with Sausage Stuffing
Parsnip Soufflé II   Glazed Onions   Giblet Gravy
Pear and Cranberry Relish
Buttered Mashed Potatoes   Red Cabbage Black Forest

Mince Pie   Pumpkin Pie   Deep Dish Apple Pie
Hard Sauce
Fruits   Nuts   Raisins en Branche

I would suggest a Chablis with the oysters, a red Bordeaux with the turkey and Madeira with the desserts.

HOLIDAYS GREAT AND SMALL

VENISON PÂTÉ

Serve this pâté cold with Melba-thin buttered rye toast.

4 slices bacon
1 bay leaf
2 pounds coarsely ground venison
1 onion, minced
1 cup roasted chestnuts, coarsely chopped
1 stalk celery, finely chopped
4 sprigs parsley, finely chopped
2 eggs
½ teaspoon dried rosemary
3 slices stale whole-wheat bread, crumbled
½ apple, peeled and chopped
⅔ cup port wine
1 clove garlic, crushed
salt and freshly ground black pepper to taste

Preheat oven to 375° F.

Line an ovenproof loaf pan with the strips of bacon and place the bay leaf in the pan. Mix the other ingredients well with a fork or with your hands. Press firmly into the pan and bake for 45 minutes. Remove to a cool place, cover with foil and put a brick or other heavy weight on top to pack it firmly.

PICKLED WALNUTS

2 (½-PINT) JARS

1 pound English walnut pieces
½ cup dark-brown sugar
2 cups maple syrup
1 cup apple vinegar
½ teaspoon each ground cloves, ginger and mace
grated rind of 1 lemon
2 jiggers dark rum

Simmer together all of the ingredients except the nuts and rum until the sauce is well thickened, about 10 minutes. Add the nuts and rum and simmer 10 minutes longer. Seal in jars while still hot. This is excellent served with game.

PARSNIP SOUFFLÉ II

2-QUART SOUFFLÉ

3 cups puréed seasoned parsnips
2 tablespoons butter
½ cup heavy cream
4 eggs, separated
sliced almonds

Preheat the oven to 375° F.

Beat together the parsnips, butter and cream. Beat the egg whites until they form stiff peaks. Beat the yolks until thick and lemon-colored. Beat the yolks into the parsnip mixture, then fold in the whites. Pour into a buttered 2-quart soufflé dish; top with sliced almonds and bake until puffed and golden brown, about ½ hour.

PEAR AND CRANBERRY RELISH

SERVES 12

1 quart cranberries, washed and picked over
¾ cup sugar
grated rind of 1 orange
juice of ½ orange
2 pears, cored, peeled and quartered
½ jigger Poire William

Put the berries, sugar and orange rind plus the juice into a food processor equipped with the steel blade. Pulse and scrape down the bowl until berries are partly minced. Add the pears last and whirl until minced but do not allow the mixture to become a purée. Add the William liqueur. Stir thoroughly and chill before serving.

RED CABBAGE BLACK FOREST

SERVES 8–10

Glorious on a cold night with turkey, red meat or game, I remember this as it used to be served at Humpelmeyer's in Munich with young venison in front of their roaring fire.

1 head red cabbage
6 tablespoons red currant vinegar
6 tablespoons sugar
1 teaspoon salt
pepper to taste
butter to taste

Wash and shred a fine head of red cabbage and place in a large pot with a little water, the vinegar, sugar, salt and pepper. Cover closely and steam, stirring occasionally, until the cabbage is just soft. Serve with butter.

Christmas Dinner

FOR 10–12

with cocktails:
Cucumber Fingers, Melba-thin Buttered Bread,
Celery   Olives   Smoked Turkey

Cream of Oyster Soup

Roast Prime Ribs of Beef au Jus
Yorkshire Pudding   Horseradish Sauce
Purée of Lima Beans and Watercress   Mélange of Vegetables
Purée of Chestnuts   Brussels Sprouts   Creamed Onions
Currant Jelly

English Plum Pudding Flambé
Foamy Apricot Sauce

Sherry with the soup, with the roast a fine claret and with the pudding, champagne.

CREAM OF OYSTER SOUP

This smooth, rich soup is only lightly flavored so that the lovely oysters can prevail.

3 tablespoons sweet butter
2 tablespoons minced shallots
3 level tablespoons flour
1½ quarts half and half
1 quart oysters
2 teaspoons sea salt
1 tablespoon green peppercorns
fresh dill

Melt the butter and add the shallots. Cook, gently, then add the flour and stir to make a *roux*. Slowly add the half and half, stirring, and cook until smooth. Drain the oysters and add their liquor to the mixture, stirring again until smooth. Add the salt and peppercorns. Beard the oysters, cut them in pieces and add to the soup. Simmer for just 3 minutes. Garnish the soup with finely snipped dill and serve.

ROAST PRIME RIBS OF BEEF AU JUS

A prime standing rib roast of beef is the joint held in the highest esteem by the Anglo-Saxon school of cooking and, quite simply, I think the most satisfactory Christmas dinner that one can have is planned around it.

Have your butcher remove the chine (backbone), short ribs, and backstrap from a 4-rib roast and tie it together. If the meat has been refrigerated let it stand at room temperature for 2 or 3 hours before roasting.

This peerless formula for cooking roast beef was perfected by Mrs. Thomas Felder, one of East Hampton's greatest hostesses and cooks and my very good friend. It produces a roast that is crusty-brown on the outside, evenly rare and juicy within.

1 (4-rib) standing rib roast (trimmed weight will be about 11–12
  pounds)
salt and freshly ground pepper to taste
flour

Preheat the oven to 500° F.

Place the roast, fat side up, on a rack in a shallow roasting pan. Rub well with salt, pepper and flour. Place in the oven (you must be sure that the oven door is absolutely tight) and roast for 15 minutes per rib, in this case exactly 1 hour. Turn off the heat but do not open the oven door for 2 hours. If you like better-done beef increase cooking time for the 4-rib roast by 15 minutes. Remove the roast to a hot platter and serve surrounded with Yorkshire Pudding cut in squares.

YORKSHIRE PUDDING

4 eggs
2 cups milk
2 cups flour
½ teaspoon salt
2 tablespoons butter
¼ cup beef drippings

Preheat oven to 450° F.

Beat together the eggs, milk, flour and salt to make a batter. Do not over-beat. It should be lumpy. Grease a roasting pan with the butter and beef drippings and turn in the batter. Bake for about 30 minutes, until the pudding is puffy and golden brown. Cut in squares and arrange around a roast of beef.

HORSERADISH SAUCE

ABOUT 1½ CUPS

½ pint heavy cream, whipped
1 (6-ounce) bottle horseradish, drained
1 tablespoon vinegar
½ teaspoon dry mustard

Beat together all ingredients and serve cold with roast beef or corned beef.

PURÉE OF LIMA BEANS AND WATERCRESS

10 OR MORE SERVINGS

This smooth bright-green purée makes an interesting use of our old friend the lima bean. In menu planning it can, on occasion, be used as an interesting substitute for potatoes.

2 boxes frozen lima beans
salt
1 bunch watercress
½ cup heavy cream
3 tablespoons butter
white pepper

Cook the lima beans in boiling salted water until tender. Drain them. Wash the watercress and remove the large stems. Purée the vegetables together until very smooth. Add the cream and butter and purée again. Season to taste with salt and white pepper.

MÉLANGE OF VEGETABLES

This method of preparing vegetables can be used in any quantity. It is a crisp and interesting way to use reliable winter vegetables.

equal quantities of carrots, green beans, zucchini and tender celery
    stalks
salt and pepper
butter

Cut the vegetables in hair-thin julienne strips and cook until barely tender in rapidly boiling water. Drain and toss with salt, pepper and butter.

PURÉE OF CHESTNUTS

Excellent served with venison as well as with roast beef. Chestnut purée is so rich that only small portions are needed.

1 (12-ounce) can of Raffetto chestnuts in brine
1 tablespoon butter
1 teaspoon salt
freshly ground white pepper
½ pint heavy cream

Drain the chestnuts and purée them in the food processor. Place in a saucepan with the butter, salt and pepper. Cook over low heat, adding the cream slowly and stirring all the time, until the purée comes to a boil. Remove from the stove and serve hot.

ENGLISH PLUM PUDDING FLAMBÉ

SERVES 12–16

1 loaf stale bread with crusts
½ pound suet, chopped
½ pound mixed candied fruit, chopped
½ cup chopped pecans or walnuts
2 cups (1 box) raisins
2 cups (1 box) currants
grated rind of 1 lemon
1 tablespoon ground cinnamon
1½ teaspoons ground ginger
1 teaspoon ground mace or nutmeg
½ teaspoon ground allspice
½ cup cherry jam
1 teaspoon salt
½ cup brandy
6 eggs, well beaten

Crumb the bread into a large bowl and add the other ingredients. Turn the batter into a well-greased 2-quart mold which has a tight lid, filling it ¾ full. (There will be a little batter left over with which you can make a small "trial" pudding.) Cover with the lid. Place on a rack in a kettle in 1½ inches of boiling water, cover and steam for 4–5 hours, adding more water if needed. Remove mold to a wire rack, uncover and allow to cool.

Add more brandy to the pudding and wrap it in plastic film or in foil. It may be stored for several weeks in a cool place.

When you are ready to use the pudding, add more brandy and again steam the pudding, covered with its lid in a kettle, for about ½ hour. Unmold it onto a large hot platter, decorate it with holly and pour another tot of heated brandy over it. Touch a match to the pudding and serve it encircled with blue-and-orange flames. Pass the Foamy Apricot Sauce with it.

FOAMY APRICOT SAUCE

ABOUT 2 CUPS

1 egg
½ package (½ pound) confectioners' sugar
1 cup heavy cream, whipped
2 tablespoons apricot jam
1 tablespoon apricot brandy
½ teaspoon vanilla extract
pinch salt

Beat the egg until thick and lemon-colored. Add the sugar gradually, sieving it if it is lumpy, and fold in the whipped cream and other ingredients. Serve in a chilled silver bowl.

New Year's Eve Supper

After the holiday feasting, something light and pretty is the most agreeable way to salute a slender New Year.

Les Oeufs de Poule au Caviar   *Hot Buttered Toast Fingers*
Roast Capon with Morelle Sauce
Wild Rice Casserole
Belgian Endive Salad
Watercress Dressing (see Index)

Bombe au Cassis (see Index)

with coffee:
Chocolate Truffles

Saratoga Water and Dom Perignon throughout, and a Happy New Year to all!

LES OEUFS DE POULE AU CAVIAR

SERVES 8

8 large eggs
2 tablespoons Crème Fraîche (see Index)
2 teaspoons finely minced onion
1 teaspoon minced chives
salt and pepper
1 tablespoon sweet butter
2 ounces caviar

Carefully remove the ends of the eggs. Empty 6 of them into a bowl, reserving the other 2 for another purpose. Wash the eggshells well and invert on a towel to dry.

Beat together the eggs with the cream, onions, chives and a little salt and pepper and scramble them in the butter over very low heat until smooth and glossy. Arrange the eggshells in egg cups; spoon mixture into them. Place a small coffee spoonful of caviar on each and the egg cap on top, allowing the caviar to peek out.

ROAST CAPON WITH MORELLE SAUCE

SERVES 8

1 capon (8–10 pounds)
salt, white pepper and paprika
butter
2 ounces dried morelles
water
flour
white wine
cognac
parsley and cherry tomatoes for garnish

Preheat the oven to 325° F.

Wash and dry the capon and rub it well, inside and out with salt, white pepper and paprika. Then rub the exterior with butter. Truss the bird, place a piece of aluminum foil lightly over it and roast, breast side up until tender, about 3 hours. Remove the foil for the last half hour of roasting. Remove the bird from the pan and keep it warm while preparing the sauce and the tomatoes. It will be easier to carve if it rests for 15 or 20 minutes.

MORELLE SAUCE

Soak the dried morelles in water for an hour. After removing the capon from the pan in which it was cooked add the water in which the morelles were soaked and 2 or 3 tablespoons of flour to the pan and stir to make a smooth sauce. Add white wine and cognac to the sauce, and then the morelles. Serve in a sauceboat with the capon. Garnish with parsley and cherry tomatoes.

WILD RICE CASSEROLE

4 cups cooked wild rice (see Index; double recipe)
2 onions, finely chopped
butter
1 pound sliced mushrooms
10 strips bacon, fried crisp and crumbled
4 chicken livers, cooked and cubed
2 cups heavy cream
parsley, for garnish

Preheat oven to 350° F.

Cook the wild rice according to the directions (*see Index*). Sauté the rice in butter in a large frying pan. Remove to a casserole and sauté the onions in more butter in the same pan. Combine all of the ingredients in the casserole and bake for 10–15 minutes. Garnish with finely chopped parsley.

INDEX

Key Lime, 226
Pastry for Double-Crust, 33
Pecan, 225
Pheasant, 174–76
Rhubarb, 32–33
Steak and Kidney, 176–77
Strawberry, 168
Veal and Ham, 177
Pineapple Mousse, Fresh, 37
Pinot Noir wine, 174
Plum Pudding Flambé, 244–45
Poires en Croûte with Caramel Sauce,
    114–15
Popovers, 23
    Blueberry, 43
Pork
    Bangers Braised in Beer, 185–86
    with Roast Potatoes; Roast Stuffed Loin
        of, 110–11
    Sausages, 186–87
    Stuffed Crown Roast, 213
Port wine, 174
Potage Forestière, 109
Potato(es)
    Allumette, 209
    Colcannon, 214
    Dilled New (menu item), 28, 75
    Herbed Mashed (menu item), 131
    Risolées, 137
    Salad with Herbs and Bacon; Hot New,
        187
Pot Roast, Park Avenue, 147
Prawns, Dublin Bay, 211
Preferitos, 197
Pre-Theater Snacks. See Snacks
Prosciutto with Figs, 80
Prunes, Stuffed, 111
Punch, Coffee, 62
Purée
    of Broccoli with Broccoli Flowerets, 106
    of Chestnuts, 243
    of Four Vegetables, 210
    of Lima Beans and Watercress, 243

Quail Eggs (menu item), 185

Rabbit, Southern Mustard, 222–23
Raspberry(ies)
    with Powdered Sugar and Crème Fraîche,
        (menu item), 80
    Shortcake; Fresh, 43
    Vinaigrette Sauce, 95
Red Burgundy wine, 108
Red Cabbage Black Forest, 238
Red Wine Basil Vinaigrette Sauce, 45
Relish, Pear and Cranberry, 237
Reuschler, Sarah Y., 160
Rhine wine, 80
Rhubarb Pie, 32–33
Rice
    Ring, 124
    White, 184
    Wild, 86–87

Wild Rice Casserole, 249
    Wild Rice Salad, 196
Roast Capon with Morelle Sauce, 247–48
Roast Long Island Duckling with Sauce
    Bigarade, 85
Roast Pheasant, 204
Roast Prime Ribs of Beef au Jus, 241
Roast Stuffed Loin of Pork with Roast
    Potatoes, 110–11
Rolled Toast, 76
Romantic Dinners. See Small dinners

Sage Derby cheese (menu item), 190
St. Patrick's Day Dinner Menu, 211–16
St. Valentine's Day Dinner Menu, 202–7
Salad dressings
    Anchovy, 42
    Blue Cheese (menu item), 160
    Farmer Cheese, 189
    Walnut Oil, 188
    Watercress, 154
Salad(s)
    Basil and Tomato (menu item), 164
    Bibb Lettuce and Walnut, 149
    Caesar, 167
    Carrot and Yogurt, 144
    Crisp Cucumber Aspic, 189
    Endive, with Brie or Camembert, 95
    Hot New Potato Salad with Herbs and
        Bacon, 187
    Irish Flag, 215
    Salade Argenteuil, 45
    Salade aux Haricots Verts, 156
    Salade Variée, 153
    Spinach, with Anchovy Dressing, 42
    Warm Spinach (menu item), 158
    Watercress (menu item), 145
    Watercress and Endive (menu item), 160
    Wild Rice, 196
    Young Lettuce with Herbs, Dressed with
        Cream (menu item), 31
Salade Argenteuil, 45
Salade aux Haricots Verts, 156
Salade Variée, 153
Sandwiches, 50, 51, 69–70
    Chicken Forcemeat, 51
    Croques, 229
    Cucumber (menu item), 50
    Filbert Butter (menu item), 50
    Ginger Marmalade with Cream Cheese
        (menu item), 50
    Guava Jelly with Cream Cheese (menu
        item), 50
    Mushroom (menu item), 50
    nut, 70
    Pecan Butter (menu item), 50
    serving suggestions, 50
    Smoked Salmon with Whipped Cream
        Cheese, 50, 70
    suggestions for, 50
    Toasted Almond, 122
    Toasted Almonds with Cream Cheese
        (menu item), 50
    Toasted Chive, 117